SEMANTICS

SEMANTICS

The Nature of Words and

Their Meanings

by HUGH R. WALPOLE

New York
W · W · NORTON & COMPANY · INC ·
Publishers

First Edition

PRINTED IN THE UNITED STATES OF AMERICA
FOR THE PUBLISHERS BY THE VAIL-BALLOU PRESS, INC.

TO ELLEN

CONTENTS

ACKNOWLEDGMENTS

THIS book owes its existence to the works of C. K. Ogden and I. A. Richards, to whom I am also deeply grateful for very generous help and encouragement in this and other ventures. They must not, however, be blamed for anything I have done to their subject.

I am indebted to the Payne Fund for help in many ways; to Charlotte Tyler Siepmann and the Orthological Committee for permission to use the materials in Chapter Nine; and to the authors and publishers who have allowed me, in my last chapter and in its appendix, to use passages from the following books.

Men Must Act, Lewis Mumford (Harcourt, Brace). *Word Economy*, L. W. Lockhart (Kegan Paul). Introduction to *The Basic Writings of Sigmund Freud*, A. A. Brill (Modern Library). *The Human Machine*, John Y. Dent (Alfred A. Knopf). *The Evolution of Physics*, A. Einstein and L. Infeld (Simon and Schuster). *Seven Types of Ambiguity*, William Empson (Harcourt, Brace). *A People's History of England*, A. L. Morton (Random House). —— *shall not perish from the earth*, James Barton Perry (Vanguard).

Das Kapital (Modern Library). *Lady Chatterley's Lover* (Alfred A. Knopf). *The Basic Writings of Sig-*

mund Freud (Modern Library). *Mein Kampf* (Houghton Mifflin). *The Philosophy of Plato* (Modern Library). *The Philosophy of Spinoza* (Modern Library). *Selections from Aristotle* (Charles Scribner's Sons). *The Doctrine of the Golden Mean* (The Commercial Press, China).

INTRODUCTION

EVERY book worth reading is a meeting place. Some would call it a battleground: are the writer's ideas or the reader's preconceptions to survive? Others more shrewdly will think of a marriage: which characteristics will prevail in whatever conceptions ensue? This book is about this meeting of minds through words. It sketches the conditions of communication; and so has to put the theory of Metaphor very much in the forefront. And of all the metaphors with which man has tried to picture the transmission of ideas, by far the best is that which too often lies dormant in the word "conceive" itself. If we think it through far enough we may come to wonder if this "metaphor" is not rather a theory awaiting development—a conception which has yet to be born, as important perhaps as its long gestation in the human intellect might suggest.

It is present in all talk of fertile ideas, seeds of thought, culture, and such. It recurs in Plato with a frequency and a frankness which embarrassed his nineteenth-century translators. It has haunted historians of ideas ever since. Perhaps today, with our increased knowledge of the detail of biological and intellectual inheritance, we are approaching a stage at which it could be further ex-

11

plored. When it is, the two sorts of conceivings are not likely to be found very different in complexity. As events in themselves they must be equally incomprehensible, but their dependencies upon other events—through the contexts Mr. Walpole lucidly treats of—seem similar.

We must, though, avoid one misunderstanding. The last words of my first paragraph might invite it. I am not talking here of "a conception in general"—the sort of thing that is "in the air" or "in the tradition," as we say— but of the individual coming into being of a capacity in the individual mind. This distinction is that between *type* and *token* explained by Mr. Walpole in Chapter Seven. The risk for the historian of ideas and for the general reader alike is that in all this he thinks of ideas as *types,* not as *tokens* of them. It is as *types* that our ideas make us acceptable or not in society. But it is by their quality or breeding as tokens formed in our minds that we are saved or lost.

If we keep this conception of conception in view, we will be less ready to suppose that any idea can be new: its novelty will be in the combinations within it; less ready to expect two men's ideas to be quite the same; less ready to dream that an idea may be simply handed from one mind to another: it has to grow there under different conditions, more or less favorable; less ready, again, to imagine that a word is a sort of cellophane container preserving a "content" intact—the same content always. Ideas are organisms and do things: different things in different conditions. We are less ready, that is, to support such views *on reflection,* for in fact they are current as perhaps never before among persons of alleged education. Semantics is perhaps most compendiously described as the attempt to generate better notions on these points, and it may be worth asking why such an attempt should be needed today more than ever.

Three reasons suggest themselves. First, the place of neatly-rounded-off scientific and technical "subjects" in our instruction. With elementary physics and chemistry, if anywhere, the above notions of ideas as static things to be imparted and applied as received seems reasonable. Technical vocabularies come as near as may be to a "one word—one idea" ideal. A view of language and thought which *is* partly true of these subjects has been spread to cover the rest. We are only now realizing what a poor instrument of general education this linguistic peculiarity makes them. They give little training in the most necessary arts of communication, through fluid and shifting words.

Second might come the unprecedented modern *scatter* of school and college subjects. Most competent educators are at one on this. We have no common body of knowledge—*acquired and developed through words*—to serve as shared starting points, landmarks, and routes of maneuver (see Chapter Four below) in our attempts to understand one another. We have not made the same mistakes together over the same pages or remedied them by the same means together. There is no guessing nowadays what anyone may happen not to know; what he therefore may be unable to understand.

Thirdly, strict translation has been vanishing from our curricula. No other exercise with language will take its place. One of the promises of Basic English on which Mr. Walpole admirably insists is that such translation from one form of English into another—with its double "incidence" on our language—will, in good teachers' hands, fill this gap.

But translation is no mere formal training in the general arts of verbal understanding and expression. It is the unique opportunity and device for intensive study. Its service to us in the past has largely been that it put great utterances of our tradition before us and kept them before us long enough for them to enter into a living connection with our thoughts, forcing us to explore them far enough to make them ours. Coleridge used to list casual reading among the great destroyers of intellects. There is no little reason to fear he was right.

Now semantics—to give yet another description of it—is the rationale of translation. It explores theoretically all the problems which come up when we compare two ways of saying the same thing. When and how may they not be "saying the same thing"? It finds, inevitably, that in the formula both "saying" and "the same thing" are radically ambiguous. Its task is to see why they must be so and how to control, as well as we may, the resultant troubles. And its prime concern—since our lives are limited—is to help us with the most important things, with the words we use in saying them, typically with such a word as "important." What may "important" mean? And which are "the most important things"?

The dictionary will send us on a long tour of such other words as "value," "good," "beautiful," "necessary," "essential," "true," "existence," "nature," "God," "love," "soul," "knowledge," "right," and "duty." But the list of their most routine connections which enough work with the dictionary might give us would be no very great help to understanding unless we brought that understanding with us. In a modest way, by knowing the English language—to some degree—we know these connections already and have some understanding. How may we get more? By consulting the best philosophers? Good, but the difficulty then is that we would have to learn to read them and of all writers they are the easiest to misread. Their pages are fuller than any others of invitations to semantic incompetence. They need in their reader a suppleness, an imaginative tolerance, a freedom and skill in shifting his assumptions and experimenting with varied viewpoints which nothing in our education today provides—certainly *not* an ordinary course in philosophy. Without all this we find them violently at variance about the meanings they seem to give to all the words to which the dictionary article on "important" would lead us. And most modern philosophers are too busy accusing one another of misunderstanding them to have any attention to spare for us or our inquiries.

It was this observation which prompted *The Meaning of Meaning*. It explains Mr. Ogden's and my preoccupation there with the mutual miscomprehension of philosophers. It explains, too, our hope that a habit of multiple definition and practice in English-English translation might make it easier to come to grips with questions—such as "What makes what important?"—which the traditional combativeness of philosophy was neglecting. To us, "meaning" itself was the supreme example, the very knot of the tangle, which was defeating and must, while it was disregarded, frustrate inquiry. Our suggested remedy—though we preferred another name, then less limited—was "semantics," a radical inquiry into the modes and causes of verbal misunderstanding. But, as Mr. Walpole wittily remarks, "this subject can be turned to very queer ends by people who already had a gleam in their eye before they met it." A publisher once told me that any book with the word "meaning" even once in its title gets a peculiar "fan mail." We did not foresee that we might encourage anyone to suppose that the great words, those with the most meanings of the most different orders, those therefore most in need of study, were to be dismissed as without meaning. Bentham's handy label, "Fictions," may have been a mistake in tactics. "Some enthusiasts," writes Mr. Walpole, "suggest throwing them away. I would like to see them try—they might as well try to split atoms with bows and arrows!"

The great words are indeed as indispensable to in-

tellectual analysis as atoms are in physics and as fundamental to intellectual order. If we can go inside them
that does not discredit them—rather the reverse. But
they are more important than this. If we distinguish emotive from referential modes of meaning (see Chapter
Two)—and there are many ways of doing this, suited to
different purposes—that is not to say that the emotive
meanings are less necessary to us or can be dismissed as
rhetoric or mere suasion. For these emotive meanings
have to do with, in fact sustain, the order in our minds,
an order not less essential to them than any contrasted
referential order. They sustain the order of our purposes.
Without that order reason and desire destroy one another. In Plato's figure, it is the whole soul—not the intellect alone—which has to be turned round toward the
idea of the good if it is to see the truth. As Mr. Walpole
well says, "Just as primitive words made us better than
animals, these great words will make us better than ourselves"—in the measure in which we rightly conceive
their meanings.

I said at the start that a book might be a battleground:
will the writer's ideas or his reader's preconceptions win?
Sometimes a passing season of the climate of opinion
seems to decide that. Semantics in the modern guise developed in the aftermath of World War I. A disillusioned
world found in it hints for discrediting further the very
things which it was already betraying. A generation was
taught only to suspect whole ranges of language it had
never studied, and these the most important to its well-

being. "Emotive language" became something to be looked down upon by these naïve sophisticates, and the moral structure of the general purposes seemed to be falling apart. There were many causes for this—chief among them, perhaps, a crude economic determinism. Some of those who noted what was happening blamed a "materialism" of which they thought semantics was an outcome. I think they were doubly wrong. Neither materialism nor any other ism is a necessary foundation for, or result of, semantics. Its aim and outcome should be the fuller understanding of *all* the doctrines—often so different—hidden beneath these large, stultifying, philosophic names. And, again, no great doctrine—well understood—destroys the moral order. Badly understood, any doctrine will: witness the materialism of Stalin and the idealism of Mussolini. What is most to be feared is general inability to understand any of the great words in any but their lowlier uses. And it is from that rising threat that semantics would chiefly guard us.

I commend this book as an introduction to its pursuit and as a very timely corrective of such misconceptions. Above all, I commend it for its insistence on the tentative exploratory nature of the study. Writings on semantics must share with philosophy pre-eminent dangers of being misunderstood. They are hard precisely because so many possible readings claim the use of their words. Mr. Walpole is too good a teacher to be surprised if, here and there, readers accuse him of thinking exactly what he was telling them not to think. Let them read on and remember that their gain is in the processes to which they are stirred, not in any product that could be served to them.

IVOR ARMSTRONG RICHARDS

1

WHAT IS SEMANTICS?

Those obstinate questionings
Of sense. . . . .
WORDSWORTH, *Intimations of Immortality.*

SEMANTICS, or semasiology, is the study of the meanings of words. One cannot elaborate this bald introductory sentence without plunging forthright into the subject matter of the study itself. Semantics shows how most of our words each have many meanings; and the word "semantics" itself—the name of the study of "the meaning of meaning"—is no exception. Some writers on "semantics" deal with very different matters from those which will be discussed under that name in this book. For example, Alfred Korzybski's book on General Semantics, *Science and Sanity,* enters the fields of anthropology, biology, botany, "conditional" (conditioned) reflexes, education, entomology, genetics, mathematics, logic, mathematical physics, neurology, ophthalmology, physics, physiology, and psychiatry. This grand tour tends to neglect those areas which I would regard as central.

On the other hand, some authorities who write about what I would call semantics call it by another name. Charles W. Morris, in his valuable monograph on semantics, *The Foundations of the Theory of Signs*, divides his general subject ("semiotic"—"semantics" to us) into three aspects, which he names "semantics," "pragmatics," and "syntactics." Morris gives a narrower range of meaning to "semantics" than will be given here.

When this elusive word is examined more closely, further perplexities are revealed. The topics of semantics begin to unfold. To take examples from one or two lines of thought:

The student of semantics studies words. When he tries to talk about "semantics," he uses words to talk about a word which itself talks about nothing but words. Is not this like trying to lift himself by his bootstraps? Following his example, can we expect to do anything but tie ourselves in knots? Presumably "semantics" is the name of something; but what sort of thing is it the name "of"? "Of" other words? Then what are *they* "of"? What is it —this naming relation, this property of being "of" another thing? This line of thought will oblige us to consider the Triangle of Reference, and the nature of the symbol-situation.

Again, some people talk very glibly about "semantics" when they have only the ghost of a notion of what they are talking about. When such a person discusses "semantics" with a specialist in linguistics, are the two people really using the same word? Again we are led to the symbol-situation, and to the distinction between Symbols and Signs.

Further, a word like "semantics" seems to lend itself

to a greater and more diverse variety of interpretations and misinterpretations than does a simple proper name like John Elgar Smith, or a simple general name like "house," or "flag." Why are some words more slippery than others? This question would take us far, into the consideration of the functions of language as well as of Contexts and Fictions.

Semantics is at present to be regarded as an exploration rather than a science, which rewards its students with a skill rather than a body of subject matter. Characteristic of the "semantic skill" are two important linguistic habits:

1. A constant awareness of the importance of context.
2. The practice of multiple definition.

"Context" is a word one generally uses vaguely. This book will explain why the meaning of a symbol depends on its context; and also the fact that the student of semantics must recognize three kinds of contexts.

Multiple definition is a technique for controlling the shifts and ambiguities of words. It is, as Dr. Richards says, the habit "of accompanying any definition or distinction we make use of with a set of rival definitions in the background of the mind." Explicitly, it is the practice of distinguishing as many as possible of the different shades of meaning of a troublesome or interesting word, and of defining each nuance.

Let "case" provide a simple example. It has different senses in: "a case of diphtheria," "the case for birth control," "in case of fire." One could begin a multiple definition of "case" on the basis of these three phrases alone.

1. A case is an example of a disease.
2. A case is a group of arguments in support of a belief.
3. A case is an event.

The first Practice Exercise at the end of this chapter goes a little further with this word. The reader who wishes really to understand a word, because it is focal to some discussion, or to a subject in which he is interested, will find that the practice of multiple definition will make him understand it far better than will a dictionary. Dictionary entries are too crude to be of much help in working out the finer points of semantics.

There are three steps in the process of multiple definition. First, one collects examples of different uses of the word, in their contexts. Secondly, one sorts out what seem to be "separate senses" and defines each sense. Lastly, one scans this list of different senses, which forms a map of the word, and considers how each sense is related to the totality of senses. This last operation is neglected by amateur semanticians, especially those who use semantics to "debunk." "This word we are using has three, or a dozen, or a score of different meanings. So it doesn't really *mean* anything; and what can we do about it?" Semantics of this odor is cheap and unprofitable. Useful words are like planets: they cannot fly around at will; they follow definite courses. Shifts of meaning occur in definite patterns.

Meaning-shift is of vital importance in the study of semantics. Typical patterns will be exemplified throughout this book. One other point may be mentioned here. Suppose one were examining "case," and had included its use as the name of a receptacle—"a case of beer." There would be no room for the case of beer in the process of putting the word together again. The history of this sort of case (which differs etymologically from the others), as well as its discordant sense, proves that it is inappropriate. That is the difference between a pun and an interesting shift of meaning. The punning word is an alien.

Thus far I have tried to show that semantics calls for a flexibility of mind, a sort of ability to call a spade a rose, which is not demanded by more formal subjects. This flexibility is demanded of the student before he can grasp the significance of semantics. After some study, he learns why it is as necessary in everyday life as in semasiology. One's tolerance need not depend upon emotional effort; it should rest upon intellectual conviction.

Semanticians

The history of semantics is both long and short. Perhaps it is now beginning to emerge as a science; and every science had its origins in philosophy. Some of the subject matter of semantics is as old as man, and most of it is as old as philosophy. The works of some philosophers have already been appraised for their value to the new study, but there must be a wealth of philosophical material which has not yet been exploited.

Jeremy Bentham's contributions to semantic theory

have been especially important. They have been exhaustively examined and utilized by C. K. Ogden. *Psyche,* Mr. Ogden's linguistic and psychological journal, has reviewed the linguistic contributions of philosophers from Bacon and Berkeley to Peirce, Husserl, and Carnap. Plato, Aristotle, Locke, Kant, Hegel, Bradley, and many other philosophers are rich in material which has not yet paid its toll to semantics.

But "semantics" as a word did not exist until this century. In 1900 it appeared as the title of the translation of Michel Bréal's *Essai de sémantique.* Lady Welby referred to it in her article on "Significs" in the eleventh edition of the *Encyclopaedia Britannica.* She complained that Bréal nowhere gave a "precise definition" of the word. "The term 'Significs,' " wrote Lady Welby, "may be defined as the science of meaning or the study of significance, provided sufficient recognition is given to its practical aspect as a method of mind, one which is involved in all forms of mental activity, including that of logic. . . . Significs includes 'Semantics,' a branch of study which was formally introduced and expounded in 1897 by Michel Bréal, the distinguished French philologist, in his *Essai de sémantique.*"

The history of semantics lies in the future. It plays an essential role in H. G. Wells's *Shape of Things to Come.* "An interesting and valuable group of investigators," wrote Mr. Wells in one chapter, "appeared first in a rudimentary form in the nineteenth century. The leader of this group was a certain Lady Welby, who was frankly considered by most of her contemporaries as an unintelligible bore. She corresponded copiously with all who would attend to her, harping perpetually on the idea that language could be made more exactly expressive, that there should be a 'Science of Significs.' C. K. Ogden and a fellow Fellow of Magdalene College, I. A. Richards (1893–1977), were among the few who took her seriously. These two produced a book, *The Meaning of Meaning*, in 1923 which counts as one of the earliest attempts to improve the language mechanism."

A Better Definition of "Semantics"

Semantics is best described by the kinds of questions it asks. You and I already have our own opinions on semantics—everyone has. We could not talk or think without having them. Semantics as a study inspects certain questions and examines, explicitly, the assumptions with which we usually answer them. Socrates had a way of asking any people he met certain questions; and before they knew it they were deep in philosophical argument. This was the Greek philosopher's method of showing men what they really thought. Many of his acquaintances would change their opinions after Socrates had made them face the assumptions on which those opinions were based.

A cluster of questions about words might be posed by a modern Socrates:

What can we learn without language? Does an animal interpret a word in anything like the same way we do?

When we say that semantics is "the study of the meanings of words," what do we *mean* by "meanings"? And what is a word? Is "postal telegram" two words? Is "postman" only one word? And what about "post-office" —one or two? Is "not" a word? If so, is the "im" in "improbable"? Is "like" a word? If so, is "sheeplike" two words? And how many words is "sheepishly"?

Who decides how many words there are in "mailbox" or "mail-box" or "mail box"? Can such a question be settled absolutely, or does it depend on different points of view, or upon different definitions of the word "word"?

Suppose we decide that "word," at least, is a word. Of what does the word consist? Black marks on paper? Impressions on a reader's eyes? Movements of somebody's vocal apparatus? A disturbance of the air? A vibration in the eardrums? A thought in somebody's "mind"? Many different thoughts in many different minds? Or is it none of these things, but simply a "meaning"? If so, why do we need a special word for "meaning"?

In their professional use of language, do scientists, salesmen, businessmen, poets, politicians, clergymen use language for different purposes? If so, can we distinguish these separate functions and use the knowledge to improve our own expressiveness?

Do people often use metaphors without knowing it?

Is it silly to use abstract words? Can we dispense with them?

Can we think of a single one of our activities that

would not be carried on more intelligently if we had a better understanding of how language works?

What will happen to the world if more and more of its educational systems train their scholars to distinguish informative utterances from utterances whose purpose it is to exhort, or to suggest, or to mystify, or to hypnotize? What will happen if they do not?

Reflection upon these questions is the best way I can think of to begin the study of semantics. Do not judge this book as if it were a book on philosophy, or logic, or mathematics. Do not expect it to proceed brick upon brick, as if a wall were being built. This subject has its own logic, and its own functions, which are concerned less with accumulated facts than with the refinement of capacities and knowledge which we all possess. Semantics is a "workout" rather than a subject.

The Usefulness of Semantics

In the past few years, semantics has caught the interest of the general public. And the general public shows a sound instinct. Semantics is a very practical business. The common-sense aspect of it renders it as appealing to the man in the street as to the scholar. Whatever his trade, any serious reader may expect the study of semantics to profit him in three ways.

He will understand better what he hears and reads.

The average man cannot grasp what he hears. Massive psychological evidence in support of this contention would only confirm what our worldly-wise knowledge of scandal and rumor and propaganda tells us already. Considering the famous Martian broadcast incident alone, we would be justified in concluding that we are not perfectly equipped to interpret the evidence of our ears. That involuntary hoax was startlingly effective. Every quarter of an hour, the invasion was halted while an announcer told the audience that this was only a play. A twiddle of the dial either way would immediately have put the listener in auditory contact with more pacific performers, including Messrs. Bergen and McCarthy. At the end of the play, the audience was again reassured by Mr. Orson Welles himself: "If your doorbell rings and nobody's there, that was no Martian—it's Hallowe'en!" Yet, immediately afterwards, thousands of people were pouring forth along the roads and streets of New Jersey with wet cloths over their faces. A professor took his torch and geologist's hammer and journeyed out in search of meteorites.

Less spectacular samples of serious misunderstanding happen every day. A recent breakdown in communication took place among a learned committee whose very task it was to diagnose such breakdowns. The committee was listening to the reading of a report. In a certain phrase came the word "di-śent," which I must give in its phonetic spelling. When the whole thing had been read, a certain member of the committee said that this word had puzzled him. "When you spoke of 'our common di-śent from the tyrannies of Europe,' " he asked, "was that word d-e-s-c-e-n-t or d-i-s-s-e-n-t?" They found the place, and the whole committee went into committee over the word. But they could not agree which it should be, either from the look of the word on paper or from its meaning in its context.

We are no better at understanding what we read. "Retarded children" have a strong representation in the primary grades of our schools. Our educational curricula are cluttered with courses in "remedial reading." Nor do these measures for curing the misinterpretators seem very successful, for similar disabilities are found in every high school and every university. This is no place to go into detailed evidence, but the reader who consults the published works of E. G. Biaggini, William Gray, and I. A. Richards will be convinced that befuddled reading goes on on a grand scale in the colleges and universities of Australia, the United States, and England.

Semantics, which shows why words are coined and how they function, is a remedy. The thoughtful educator should give it a chance, whether he is concerned to improve himself or to teach his classes to read better.

He will talk and write more effectively.

Misinterpretation is only half the fault of the listener. Semantics will help speakers and writers to see why misunderstanding occurs. Familiarity with the nature of the symbol-situation should teach the speaker the difference between speech and verbosity. His study of Fictions will show him how to use simpler language when it is appropriate; and practice with the Theory of Definition will increase his skill in communicating his thoughts to a particular audience. He will be better able to convince and persuade when he understands the workings of Metaphor, and when he realizes the different jobs an utterance can do.

He will think more accurately.

This is most important of all. Now, more than ever, men need to foster and strengthen their own powers of keen and unflurried thought. They need greater powers; and they stand in danger of losing such powers as they have. Countries are at war in all five continents. Aggressive leaders, directing totally organized forces, are trying to kill the possibility of ordinary men ever being men again.

And today a world at peace would still be a world in danger. Our minds have not kept pace with the almost inconceivable changes in our physical means of transport and communication. Less than fifty years has seen the birth of the Diesel engine, the airplane, moving pictures, wireless telegraphy, radio, telephotography, and television. The earth shrinks rapidly under our feet. A period of time which a century ago would have been consumed while the Londoner was traveling to Bath is now sufficient to take the New Yorker to Moscow. And we no longer have to go to a place in order to hear it— to see it, even. Soon everyone will have the possibility of almost instantaneous communication with everyone else on earth. Two thousand million pairs of ears and eyes, ripe to be swayed; and the forces that want to sway them will not bother to pause every fifteen minutes to warn their audience not to take them literally.

The time will come when educators will co-operate in the task of arming their peoples against the dangers of misreading and half-hearing. That, perhaps, must wait for the suppression of those riding masters who sweat to be conquerors. In the meantime the individual will try to clarify his own thoughts, to "cultivate his own garden." Semantics will help him to think more accurately because, by showing how words and thoughts are connected, it helps one to draw the line between verbal and mental problems. He will be less *dependent* on words, better able to concentrate on thoughts, whatever their verbal clothing.

I hope the reader feels dissatisfied with this chapter. Semantics is not an "easy" subject; and any short introduction which claimed to cover the water front would deserve suspicion. I have merely tried to give the feel of the subject. The next chapter will discuss propaganda, in the course of a general treatment of the different functions of language. After an analysis of the four different jobs an utterance can do, a general distinction is made between the language of fact and the language of emotion. Thereafter, for the most part, the book concerns itself with "referential" language. The third chapter deals with the Sign, as a unit of learning and interpretation in animals as well as in men. This leads to the consideration of the Symbol, a kind of sign taken to be peculiar to the human species. Symbolic interpretation is treated as a refinement of sign interpretation. This fourth chapter is the core of the book.

After this description of symbols, it is shown how the "meaning" of a symbol depends upon its Context; and further that the student of semantics must recognize three different kinds of contexts. The next topic is that operation which we call Definition, which consists of the linking up of two different parts of a context—or, to put it in another way, of merging two contexts into a larger one.

As I have said, the fourth chapter describes the process of naming simple objects, or Referents; and the next two chapters are concerned with the referents in their contexts, which may be regarded as complex referents. Chapters 7 and 8 examine a further sort of complication, in which the referent is treated "as if" it were some other referent. It is shown that all the eccentricities of metaphors and Fictions exist embryonically in the behavior of the symbol in a normal symbol-situation.

The last two chapters describe skills by which the reader may turn his knowledge of the theory of semantics to practical use. Throughout the book, however, there are Practice Exercises after each chapter. The reader is asked to work with them on his way through the book. They save a great deal of statement and restatement about matters of theory. By solving them according to his best judgment, and by seeing how the exercises are connected with their chapters, the reader supplies links which serve instead of endless chains of words about words about . . . etc. I suggest a special notebook for these exercises: partly because some of them serve elsewhere in the book as references and examples, and partly because I think the reader will sometimes be intrigued to see how he changes his mind about his solutions. I would be grateful for suggestions for improving these exercises; but, as they stand, they are an integral part of the book.

Chief Points

Semantics is interested in the *senses* of words, and is of general value because it gives a better knowledge of what one is doing every time one makes use of language. It may best be looked upon, not as a complete science, but as a body of questions touching upon the connections between language and thought. By guiding one through these questions of theory, it gives a knowledge which may be put to use and which will have as its outcome clearer thought, better writing, and sharper reading.

Practice Exercises

I

Case.—Each of the sentences below contains the word "case." Put beside *each* sentence in *B* the number of the *A* sentence which comes nearest to using the word in the same sense.

A. 1. I thought he was in Mexico; but such was not the case.

2. In this case the detective was completely baffled.

3. "You have a very good case," said the lawyer. 6, 5

4. What is the case of this pronoun? 2

B. 1. In case of sickness, fill in Form A3. ....

2. The Latin adjective agrees with the noun in gender, number, and case. 4

3. Dr. Johnson had a case of diphtheria on his hands. 2 ....

4. If this was the case, why didn't you inform the police? 1

5. The Case of the Stolen Necklace was not solved quickly. 3

6. He stated his case badly. ...3....

II

Body.—Each of the sentences below contains the word "body." Put beside *each* sentence in B the number of the A sentence which comes nearest to using the word in the same sense.

A. 1. Exercise helps to keep the body healthy.

2. The doctor viewed the body.

3. His limbs were short, but he was very long in the body.

4. The tires were flat, the mudguards were twisted, and the body was smashed.

5. Put your information in the body of the letter.
6. Through associating with lawyers, he has picked up a considerable body of legal knowledge.
7. The Scottish landlady was a comfortable, honest old body.
8. A body of armed men attacked the City Hall.
9. The doctor said, "There is a foreign body in your eye."
10. They spent four or five hours studying the heavenly bodies through a telescope.

B. 1. We went in a body to see the President. . . . .
2. O'er shady groves they hover,
And with leaves and flowers do cover
The bodies of unburied men. . . . .
3. Gin a body meet a body
Coming through the rye. . . . .
4. I am absent in body, but present in spirit. . . . . . .
5. Soul is form, and doth the body make. . . . .
6. He concentrated his attention on the body of the argument. . . . .
7. Joe sent a left to the jaw, and a right to the body.
. . . .
8. Nobody knows where he's gone. . . . .

III

True

A. 1. If I believe it strongly enough, then it is true.
2. The last witness had given a true description of the incident.

    3. The scientist said that though his colleague's theory did not, as far as he knew, contradict the facts he could not accept it as true.

B. 1. Say what's true, and shame the Devil. . . . .

    2. All things which are beautiful are true. . . . .

    3. The true story of that expedition was never revealed. . . . .

    4. Everything you see is not necessarily true. . . . . . .

Note: For all these exercises, put two or more numbers in cases where you are doubtful, or where the word in question seems to have more than one sense within its context.

Get someone else to do these and all similar exercises, and then try to discover the reasons for disagreements. There is not always one "right" answer.

2

EMOTIVE LANGUAGE:
THE LANGUAGE OF FEELING

*We need a spell of purer science and purer poetry
before the two can again be mixed, if indeed this
will ever become once more desirable.*
I. A. RICHARDS, *Principles of Literary Criticism.*

SOME years ago a dog team set out from somewhere
to carry diphtheria antitoxin to Nome, Alaska. There
were a number of hardships and obstacles, and millions
of newspaper readers got excited over the party's daily
adventures. The whole thing turned out to be a publicity stunt arranged by an American chemical firm to
advertise their diphtheria serum. In a world where prop-
agandists are so resourceful, it is up to their targets to
have a few resources too. That is one purpose of this
chapter, to provide certain criteria of judgment to serve
as instruments of self-defense: it goes back into history
in its quest for examples and illustrations, but everything
fits together into a modern application.

Toward the middle of the last century, the authorities
of a newly founded linguistic society in France rejoiced
over a recipe which they thought would stop some of
their members from talking nonsense. Section Two of
their statutes was framed to read: *La Société n'admet*

38

aucune communication concernant, soit l'origine du lan-
gage, soit la création d'une langue universelle. Thus the
society put a taboo on the discussion of two subjects: the
origin of language and the possibility of inventing a universal tongue. In taking the view that there was no
sense in trying to get at the truth on the first question,
and no possibility of any practical outcome to an in-
quiry about the second, these officials barred two of the
most fruitful and stimulating subjects available.

Among the brain waves then current concerning the
origin of speech were two which were later nicknamed
the "bow-wow" theory and the "pooh-pooh" theory. The
first theory said that early man heard (for instance) a
dog barking, and barked himself; his bark was a word,
meaning perhaps "bark" or possibly "dog," or, more probably, either or both. (It seems evident that ambiguity
came into man's life even before the serpent.) The pooh-
pooh school of thought maintained that the first words
were man's musical accompaniment to his feelings. When
one has a feeling of disgust or contempt one is apt, to
take Darwin's example, "to blow out of the mouth or
nostrils, and this produces sounds like *pooh* or *pish.*"
So these words would be the names of feelings or
emotions, and such feelings would have labels that fitted
very well for the good reason that feeling and label both
came from the same physiological source.

Emotive Language and Propaganda

There were, of course, several theories, each with

something to be said for it. These particular two are interesting here as illustrating a couple of different motives for using language. The bow-wow man reacts to, or talks about, a referent or object which is out in the world. The pooh-pooh man reacts to, or expresses, his own feelings. The two of them provide examples of two functions of language which are quite distinct. These are called the *referential* and the *emotive* functions. Emotive language expresses the speaker's feelings, and aims at stirring those of the hearer and perhaps spurring him on to some action. Referential language refers to objects or actions or situations which can be pointed to or described, and makes statements which may be verified or disproved by the other fellow. The difference between the two is the difference between a statement like "The Normandie sails at noon on Wednesday" and an expression like "My soul is a ship in full sail." Any educational system that gave training in making this distinction, especially on the basis of the fuller analysis to come later in this chapter, would provide its society with a first-rate umbrella against sales talk and propaganda.

Reference has already been made to the dangers of discussing isolated words out of their contexts, and this warning will frequently be repeated. But here the risk is taken. The reader is invited to look at the two lists of words below and to select one word from each group as being an emotive word. A word is used emotively, we remember, when the speaker uses it to reveal his own attitude toward the object about which he is talking.

Here are five nouns: building, factory, home, house, stable. And five adjectives: beautiful, electric, hard, opposite, wet. Which are the two emotive words?

The word "home" has a very strong emotional aroma about it, as the real-estate agent knows. So much so, indeed, that the French have borrowed it; and so, though the Frenchman's house, referentially speaking, is *la maison*, he speaks of it emotively as *le home*. (The reader does not need to be told that "beautiful" is the other emotive word.)

A simple experiment might interest some of those who like to examine their own language. Looking over half a dozen pages of writing they have done recently—notes, letters, reports—they might class all the words they have used under two headings. The emotive list would consist of the "nice," "wonderful," "beauty," and "goodness" kind of words, and might give the individual a bird's-eye view of his own unconscious methods of self-deception. In the other, the referential class, would be found two kinds of words: gadgets like "a," "the," "of," "for," "to," which are handy devices for tying words together into coherence; and words which seem to have some "content," some "meaning," of their own. These last are a selection from one's special mental pets, and deserve to be turned over, looked at, and taken apart. Everybody has a unique collection of words that he uses regularly, like an individual set of tools. They are fairly constant; and it is not nearly as important to acquire more of them as it is to use good judgment in choosing them and to gain a knowledge of all the different ways in which they can be worked. For we all have to arrange our thoughts, and communicate them, by means of these instruments; and those who study them are rewarded in compound interest for their time and trouble. Incidentally, such study has the result of increasing the vocabulary as well as of making it more efficient.

The common words are the ones that need our attention most. We talk glibly about souls before we have paused to get a clear idea of the different kinds of thing we can mean by the word "body." We are willing to turn our attention to the spirit while we remain weak before the task of diagnosing the behavior of the word "letter." The tools we use to think with, and to put our thoughts across to our fellows, deserve at least as much attention as the other tools of our various trades.

The functions of language must not be left basking in a light of false simplicity. Referential language is not always used in a referential way. Perhaps we may use as a warning an experience of the late G. K. Chesterton, who, while turning over in his brain schemes of his own, is said to have stopped before the stall of a fishwoman. Fixing her pleasantly with his eye, he began: "You are a noun, a verb, and a preposition." The woman blushed. Chesterton pitched his voice a note higher and continued firmly: "You are an adverb, an adjective, and a conjunction; you are a pronoun—" Pronoun was too much. The fishwoman smacked his face with a flounder and called the police.

The bulk of the words we use were originally used emotively. We can see why when we consider that human speech and human song had the same origins. Primitive men used little thought, and much sound and feeling. It is possible, with careful definition, to take emotive words and use them referentially. Writers on theories of art try earnestly to be precise in their handling of such a word as "beautiful." In ordinary conversation, on the other hand, all of us have a habit of fathering non-emotive words and using them very emotively indeed. We stretch the uses of terms we borrow from psychology —"rationalization," "complex," etc.—or from politics and economics, like "capitalist," "profit," "labor"; on a more familiar level, too, we take the names of our animals in vain. It is possible to describe the kind of treatment a word is getting only by examining it in use. If a speaker is reluctant to define one of his words, or to replace it by a substitute, he is probably using it emotively.

When civilization has been won back, this distinction between emotive and referential language, if it is not used crudely—in crude hands it does more harm than good—will improve our language and thinking. Among civilized human beings, quarrels and arguments become quite unnecessary. Arguments represent clashes of interests and should be discussed as such. It is by keeping normal discussion free from terms which are not referential that we take the first and biggest step in preventing it from degenerating into argument.

Yet civilization needs emotive language too. Poetry

is the richest kind of emotive language. While this book will not examine in detail the nature of such language— proposing more especially to deal with the referential language of work, business, science, and discussion—the author's point of view is clearly expressed in the quotation at the head of this chapter. If we could get the habit of distinguishing referential from emotive language, we would cease to expect a poet's statements to be always open to scientific verification; and we would not reject a poet as worthless because we could not agree with his religion or philosophy or politics. Nor, in the practical world, would we fall for propaganda or for high-pressure salesmanship.

One is apt to slip metaphorical plugs into one's ears and reiterate the weak cry of "don't believe anything you hear." It is better (and semantics makes it possible) to pick out and check the references and to ignore the emotions. Salesmen and leaders disapprove of such activities. Mr. Elmer Wheeler, in his celebrated *Sizzle Book* (It's the sizzle that sells the steak—not the cow), tells his salesmen readers that "What is most important to remember is that these three 'mental pocketbooks' are not in the logical front part of the prospect's mind but are buried deep in the emotional *back* part of the brain. You must fashion your words so that they will fly past the prospect's cold reasoning, his logical front mind, and move, *emotionally*, his real basic buying urges in the 'depth' of his brain." (The punctuation is Mr. Wheeler's.)

Herr Hitler knows the same thing, and expresses it in

very much the same way. His oratorical outbursts are aimed at the feelings of his hearers. He talks emotively, and knows from experience that it is best to choose the times when the logical faculties of his audience are most likely to be dull. To quote his own words: "In the morning, and during the day, men's minds are most strongly opposed to any attempt to persuade them to adopt new decisions and new opinions. But in the evening they succumb more easily to the dominating force of a stronger will. For in truth every meeting of this sort consists of a struggle between two opposing forces. The mighty oratorical talent of the masterful leader will succeed more easily in inspiring with a new will men whose powers of resistance have already been lessened by nature than if they were still in full possession of all the resources of their mind and will.

"The same end is attained by the artificial yet mysterious lighting in the Catholic churches, by the lighted candles, and incense, the censers, etc.

"In this struggle of the orator against the adversaries he wishes to convert, he gradually acquires a wonderful understanding of the psychological conditions necessary for propaganda."

Somebody should write a treatise entitled *A Semantic Study of the Decisive Speeches of History*. Then we would see how man through the ages has listened to emotive words and told himself that they persuaded his reason. The speech of Pope Urban II at Clermont still remains one of the greatest performances of all time.

The Pope addressed his audience in an impressive setting. There at Clermont were assembled cardinals with purple robes, bishops with golden *chapes,* barons and citizens from all parts of Christendom. They gathered before a platform beneath a canopy of cloth-of-gold. Then a tall man took his stand between two glittering crosses, a man who was robed in white except for the heavy pallium over his shoulders bearing tiny crosses, and the pallium was of the same hue as his thick, curling beard. He came closer to the platform, and we are told that the whole throng stirred, like a meadow in the summer breeze. Then Urban spoke, and, being a Frenchman, he spoke the Romance language rather than the harsher Latin:

"O ye men of the Franks, who live beyond the mountains! God hath favored you in many ways, in your happy land as in your steadfast faith and valor. To you our words are spoken, and by you our message will be passed on. We wish you to know what grievous cause has brought us hither, to your land, and what need has led us not only to you but to all the faithful.

"I speak to you who are present; I announce it to those who are absent, and Christ ordains it.

"From the borders of Jerusalem and the city of Constantinople, ominous tidings have gone forth. An accursed race, emerging from the kingdom of the Persians, a barbarous people, estranged from God, has invaded the land of the Christians in the east and has depopu-

lated them by fire, steel, and ravage. These invaders are
Turks and Arabs."

After the body of the speech, which was laden with
atrocity stories, came the peroration:

"Fear not torture, for therein lies the crown of martyr-
dom. The way is short, the struggle brief, the reward
everlasting. Yea, I speak now with the voice of the
prophet, 'Arm thyself, O mighty one!' Take up your arms,
valiant sons, and go. Better fall in battle than live to see
the sorrow of your people and the desecration of your
holy places."

It would be an interesting exercise to underline all
the words used emotively in the above quotation and to
substitute words which were neutral in feeling; or, better, to rewrite the whole passage restricting the paraphrase to purely referential statements. Such exercises
will be discussed in detail later.

In one chapter of *The Epic of America* the historian
specifically makes the distinction we are here discussing,
when he contrasts the reasoning of the merchants with
the emotive speeches of Sam Adams, that past master in
the art of incitement, concerning the Stamp Act:

"While the merchants were busy pointing out to their
London correspondents that the new laws would hurt
the business of all alike, Adams at once struck boldly out
to inflame the passions of the crowd by threatening that
it was to be reduced to the 'miserable state of tributary
slaves,' contrasting its freedom and moral virtue with the

tyranny and moral degradation of England. He proclaimed that the mother country was bent on bringing the colonies to a condition of 'slavery, poverty, and misery,' and on causing their utter ruin."

Our own age is not lacking in masters of emotive manipulation. I again quote Herr Hitler, this time in admiration of a war enemy.

"I read a detailed criticism of the speeches of Lloyd George (when merely Minister of Munitions) which arrived at the brilliant conclusion that these speeches were second-class from the philosophical and scientific point of view, that here we had commonplace and trivial utterances. Some time later I got hold of some of these speeches, in pamphlet form, and I could not help laughing aloud when I saw how our German penster had missed the point of these psychological masterpieces, this artistry in handling the soul of the crowd. Our man had judged these speeches exclusively from the point of view of the impression they produced upon his own sophisticated mind, while the great English demagogue had composed them with the sole aim of exercising the maximum effect over the mass of his audience, and in a wider sense the whole of the English lower classes. From this point of view, this Englishman's speeches were prodigious masterpieces."

The author of an article on propaganda in an American journal of psychology set forth at the end four rules which he thought explained the secret of successful propaganda, the first being: rely on emotion, never argue.

Involuntary support of this rule was provided by a director of propaganda for some American power companies, who said, when asked how he would work against the election of a senator who favored government ownership of utilities: "My idea would be not to try logic or reason, but to try to pin the Bolshevik idea on my opponent."

The foregoing examples and illustrations probably make clear enough the distinction between these two ways of using language. It should be explicitly added, however, that talking, especially talking emotively, is far from being a matter of words alone. The situation, the circumstances, as well as the gestures and expression of the speaker, all come into the picture. The emotive factors, especially, take many forms. Sometimes emotive speech may consist of so many words, which more or less stand on their own feet and can be looked at separately. But other examples are nothing but ritual, or social gesture—"How do you do"; "Good-by, I had such a lovely time"—and here analysis of the separate words would be wasted. Very often one gets a whole bunch of words acting as gestures, or signals, which are as much a unity as the gong which in some theaters is the signal that the curtain is going to rise, or as the deep-voiced whistle Froebel used to summon his baby pupils to a change of occupation. Intonation and "tone of voice," in speech, also come in on the emotive side. Emphasis, or stress, is another consideration; though in the English language stress also has a referential function, telling the listener which ideas need his particular attention. (For example, one can make this sentence, "She took her new green hat from that shelf," answer nine different questions, by emphasizing the different words.)

Three Aspects of Emotive Language

In view of such complications, it will be advisable to look more closely into the nature of emotive language. The secret of appreciating and criticizing any sample of speech lies in estimating how it operates these four functions of language: Sense, Feeling, Tone, and Intention. Anyone faced with the problem of explaining the effects of a work of literature or of a masterpiece of propaganda will find it easier and better to examine them under these four headings. Observe that three of them are different sides of the emotive function.

Sense is the principal factor in referential language, the language of scientific statement. Referential language just says what it says, and nobody's moods or motives come into the picture. We will give a sample of it:

"Insulin is the hormone secreted by the cells of the islands of Langerhans in the pancreas. It has been obtained as a crystalline substance by J. J. Abel, but its chemical formula is not known as yet. It is concerned with the regulation of the blood sugar oxidation in the body, a deficiency due to the destruction of the cells of the islands of Langerhans, causing diabetes. It was first extracted by C. H. Best and F. G. Banting."

This is a medical statement, though not on the technical level. You can easily think of similar statements in different fields of interest: about fishing, or bridge, or aviation, or politics, or heavy water. Such statements are examples of the language of science and of common sense.

Feeling expresses how the person speaking feels about the things he is discussing. An encyclopedist who spoke of insulin as "the cute little hormone secreted by the bonny cells of the islands of Langerhans" would be introducing the function in a way most of us would consider inappropriate. The Anglo-Indian golfing colonel who, on his arrival at Pine Valley, New Jersey, exclaimed how top-hole it was to play in such a paradise, with a lovely brook meandering its jolly little way through the course, and then at the fourteenth hole, after slicing, snarled a query about how the dickens a fellow could get a decent match when there was a sewer in the way, provides another example of the function of Feeling. The Feeling and the Tone functions find their most valuable expression in emotional literature, especially poetry. We should read more good poetry as an effective aid in retaining our sanity.

Tone is the expression of the speaker's attitude toward the person he is addressing. It is a complication we all have to allow for in our dealings with people. As speaker, any smoothly oiled citizen of the world is obliged to pay this element a good deal of attention, while the listener has to sift it out before he can get the Sense of any statement. The boss tells you that it is with great regret that he dispenses with your valuable services; the publisher tells you that undoubtedly your book has great merit, and it is highly thought of by Mr. ——, but Mr. —— ——. Tone, then, expresses what the speaker feels about his hearer. Or what the writer feels about his reader; for in the present exposition "writing" or "speaking" mostly refers to both operations.

Intention has its place in any utterance, whether it be social gossip, a novel, or a book on science, but its most obvious form is exemplified by the propagandist. He, like the rest of us, has his own feelings and interests. His way of boosting them is to incite you to do something for him. In speeches such as his, in which the Intention function is dominant, you would get a totally false view if you thought that its Sense or its Feeling meant very much to the man who made the speech. The propagandist's mind is made up. His purpose is not to get his hearers or readers to think, but to get them to think his way. And to do what he wants. Here lies the line between education and propaganda.

We can all of us think of skillful examples of propaganda in which language seems to be used in a purely referential way, although the whole utterance is made for a completely different purpose. In other words, the dominating function of these examples is the function of Intention. As social and political animals, we are to-day vitally interested in people's intentions. "What's he after?" "Who's behind it?" In the midst of the blare of publicity from salesmen, politicians, churchmen, educators, and leaders of thought, we would do well to keep our weather ear open for signs of this fourth function of language. We can always profit from any Sense there happens to be in their statements. We should, in addition, beware of the current tendency to use the word "propaganda" emotively. It would be worth while to examine the heads of those who maintain that all persuasion is equally bad, whatever courses it urges, bad or good.

Stuart Chase has written a book on the use and misuse of words and in one chapter he displays as horrible examples of misuse passages by well-known writers. After presenting a passage from one of his own earlier books, through which he scatters a whole host of blab-blabs to replace words he now disapproves of, he says, "I suspect that the paragraph was really written because I wanted church people to join with me in trying to get rid of slums, poverty and economic misery. Well, why didn't I say so?"

Intention—and one could say the same of any of the three other functions of language—is heavy in some utterances, and in others so insignificant that it can almost be ignored. Sales talks and election speeches could be found to illustrate one end of the scale, and a geometry book would exemplify the other end. In analyzing any kind of utterance, however, one must keep all four functions in mind; otherwise, one runs the risk of wandering off into other fields of study. If we wanted to discuss Intention and intentions in general, for example, we should find ourselves discussing Sociology. This last statement may be supported by a prewar message from Berlin to the New York *Times:*

"An agreement between the German and Polish education ministries, announced here today, provides that school textbooks will be revised to eliminate 'all expressions and phrases liable to offend the national feelings of either country.'

"As interpreted by the German press, the agreement should lead to a dispassionate presentation of the epochs in which the two countries opposed each other. Part of the agreement calls for deletions of texts that might be interpreted as insulting or likely to injure national sensibilities.

"Both Education Ministries will collaborate in this work. It is intended to extend the agreement to other branches of education.

"This announcement is particularly interesting in view of the report of a similar agreement between French and German historians last year, a report that was repudiated here as premature and unauthorized."

We have to expect an overdose of Intention from the history textbooks of any nation.

This completes our present analysis of the four functions of language. Nobody who uses it can fail to find it a great help. It is easy to remember and always at hand. It enables us to weigh and assess the value of any pronouncement, any specimen of praise, prayer, poetry, or prejudice to which we may be subjected. And here we shall leave the subject, lumping the three emotive functions together again and returning to our original distinction between referential language, which draws the hearers' attention to some state of affairs, and emotive language, which aims at expressing the speaker's feelings and encouraging the hearer to adopt a certain attitude. In the normal way, any bit of writing contains both kinds.

Echoes of Sound and Sentiment

It is a sad thing that many writers on semantics who make the distinction between referential and emotive language have gone around making it with a chip on their shoulder. Some of these have described emotive language as "nonsense"; and one cannot feel quite sure that the sting is taken completely away from the insult by their explanation that "nonsense" is a purely technical term, used referentially. Stuart Chase has rewritten passages from the writings of the great in paraphrase, replacing every word which ended in -ness or -ity or -tion or -ment or -ism by the less euphonious word "blab-blab." There is a danger here, because although some of the big abstract words (which, as Joyce's Stephen Dedalus said, have made us so unhappy) are emotive enough wherever they turn up, others *are* referential terms, but Fictions—with which this book will be concerned in later chapters.

"Emotive" and "Fiction" are not disparaging terms. Fictions are a linguistic necessity, and emotive language is another name for Poetry, which is a human necessity. We all have daydreams. The daydreams and castles in Spain of our inner life are a kind of private poetry. To share the poet's experiences is to enrich and refine this inner life. People like Auden, Eliot, Empson, MacLeish, Rukeyser, Spender, Yeats are fine and rich personalities communicating to their readers their reaction to today's world. The values of poetry of every age come mainly through language used emotively.

> "Drop thy pipe, thy happy pipe;
> Sing thy songs of happy cheer":
> So I sung the same again,
> While he wept with joy to hear.
>
> "Piper, sit thee down and write
> In a book, that all may read."
> So he vanished from my sight,
> And I pluck'd a hollow reed.
>
> "And I made a rural pen,
> And I stain'd the water clear,
> And I wrote my happy songs
> Every child may joy to hear."

These three verses of Blake certainly teach us nothing. They have to be read as music rather than as logic. They are language used emotively. Matthew Arnold wrote of

Byron that "He taught us nothing, but our soul has felt him like the thunder's roll."

Without trying to give an explanation of any of Blake's verses, let us loiter for a moment just to hint at the kind of richness to be savored in the enjoyment of poetry, which must be ignored in the study of referential language. For one thing, there is the physical sound of the words, together with the muscular movements that have to be made when they are spoken aloud. Try saying aloud the words "pluck" and "hollow" and see how much they can "mean" emotionally when they are said with as much "expressive" power as possible. See how the consonant which dominates the first of the above three verses suggests other words which, though absent, seem to make their presence felt: words like weep, ripe, tip, drip, lip, top, stop, drop (tears). The vowel "i" is very strong here too, with a suggestion of ideas like sigh, high (note), sky, eye, die. Other words are summoned by emotional or intellectual association, giving as the total effect of the first verse a feeling of beauty, sadness, and peace which the mere sense of the words certainly does not explain. Indeed, there is a kind of struggle between the sense and the feeling.

A detailed discussion of the enjoyment of poetry, important though it is, lies outside our scope. The same reasons which keep the businessman from reading poetry prevent him from enjoying his vacation. And even a book which is mainly concerned with language in what one might call its steering function must give a passing bow to the gasoline which makes the engine go and the oil which keeps it going smoothly.

Chief Points

There are two different uses of language, and it is necessary to keep them separate in our minds: the Emotive use and the Referential use. This book is chiefly interested in the referential language of work, business, science, and discussion.

Every example of language, in writing or in talk, may be viewed from four different angles, the reader or hearer looking in turn at its Sense, its Feeling, its Tone, and its Intention. Though to some degree all four are normally present in every statement, Feeling and Tone are specially important in poetry, and Intention in propaganda. Poetry is of great value in putting our feelings in order and giving us a healthy frame of mind.

Practice Exercises

Call me Ishmael. Some years ago—never mind how long precisely—having little or no money in my purse, and nothing particular to interest me on shore, I thought I would sail about a little and see the watery part of the world. It is a way I have of driving off the spleen and regulating the circulation. Whenever I find myself growing grim about the mouth; whenever it is a damp, drizzly November in my soul; whenever I find myself involuntarily pausing before coffin warehouses, and bringing up the rear of every funeral I meet; and especially whenever my hypos get such an upper hand of me, that it requires a strong moral principle to prevent me from deliberately stepping into the street, and methodically knocking people's hats off—then, I account it high time to get to sea as soon as I can. This is my substitute for pistol and ball. With a philosophical flourish Cato throws himself upon his sword; I quietly take to the ship. There is nothing surprising in this. If they but knew it, almost all men in their degree, some time or other, cherish very nearly the same feelings towards the ocean with me.

Moby Dick, Chapter 1, first paragraph

Above is the first paragraph of *Moby Dick,* as Herman Melville wrote it. Below are three attempts to interpret this passage by means of analytical paraphrases.

1. After carefully reading all four versions, grade the paraphrases in their order of merit. Which gets nearest to the original? Which is worst?

2. Note down one or two of what you consider the most glaring examples in these paraphrases of errors in the interpretation of Sense, of Feeling, of Tone, and of Intention.

Is it true that each paraphrase contributes in some way to a richer understanding of the original?

A. Give me the name Ishmael. Some years back—do not be troubled by detailed thoughts about how long—having little or no money in my money bag, and nothing special to be of interest to me on solid land, I had the thought of sailing about a little, to see the wet part of the earth. It is a way I have of driving off my angry

feelings, and keeping my blood system regular. Whenever I see myself getting serious about the mouth; whenever it is raining in my heart; whenever I see myself stopping automatically before death-box storehouses, and
going in back of every line of persons going to put a dead
body in the earth; and specially when my feelings get
such an upper hand of me that my strong sense of right
behavior sends me stepping into the street on purpose,
and putting men's hats off their heads one after the
other—then, I take into account that it is high time to get
to sea as quickly as possible. This does for me the work
of gun and ball. Wisely and in good form, Cato went
running onto his blade; I quietly take to the ship. There
is nothing surprising in this. If they were but conscious
of it, almost all men in their degree, some time or other,
put about the same value on the sea as I do.

B. Let my name be Ishmael. Some years back—the
year itself is not important—having little or no money,
and nothing specially interesting on land, I got the idea
of sailing about a little, and seeing some of the waters
covering the earth. It is a way I have of driving off
my bad humor, and getting my blood in good working
order. Whenever I am getting stiff about the mouth;
whenever it is a dark, wet November in my heart; whenever I get into the way of stopping unconsciously before the buildings where death-boxes are kept, and join-
ing in the street every company I see taking a friend to
his last resting place; and specially whenever my insides

get such an upper hand of me that all my self-control is needed to keep me from stepping slowly into the street, and one after another sending men's hats off their heads —then it seems to me to be quite time I went off to sea. This is in place of gun or knife or cord. In delicate harmony with the twists of his thought, Cato put the weight of his body onto the point of his blade; I quietly take to the ship. There is nothing surprising in this. If only they were conscious of it, almost all men in their degree have at some time or other very much the same feelings for the sea that I have.

C. My name is Ishmael—or that name is as good as any other. Some years back—it is not important when— having very little money, and nothing of special interest on land, I had the idea that I would get in a ship and see something of the seas. It is my way of sending away my bad humors, and getting my blood in working order. Whenever I make the discovery that my face is becoming sad; whenever there is dark wet winter weather within me; whenever I make the discovery that I am coming to an automatic stop before those places where death-boxes are stored, and whenever, when I see a line of persons in the street taking some dead man or woman to be put away, I go with them; and specially when my low condition of mind gets such control of me that I have trouble in keeping myself from stepping with a sense of purpose into the street, and regularly sending persons' hats off their heads—then I make the decision that I had better get to sea at once. This is what I put in the place of instruments of death. In a like condition, Cato put himself to death; I quietly take to the ship. There is nothing surprising in this. Though they are not conscious of the fact, about all men to some degree, at some event or time, take the same viewpoint as I with respect to the sea.

3

SIGNS: *LEARNING WITHOUT WORDS*

We can discern in the dog's mind the same essential processes that we use when we learn a language.
WELLS, HUXLEY AND WELLS, *The Science of Life.*

HAVING distinguished in the previous chapter between referential and emotive language, and having noted the dangers of using this distinction too freely, our next task is to see how language becomes "referential"; that is, how it comes to have Sense (Function 1). That task is facilitated if one keeps two general notions in the back of one's mind: first, that all the processes that we call interpretative—seeing, hearing, feeling, smelling, and so on—involve complicated physiological and psychological activities; second, and this notion has a connection with the first, that a peculiar shift of meaning characterizes the names of all such processes —the words already mentioned and others like *touch, interpretation, perception.* Since these terms all follow the same sort of shifts, it is not very helpful to discuss some of them by means of the others; we must try to get behind the causes of all such shifts. Few people find it hard to appreciate them while they are being examined, but it is strangely easy to be confused by these shifts in ordinary discussion. This chapter seeks to explain their nature and behavior, and the reasons for them.

Let us provide a framework of comparison by examining the word *sense* at three obvious points of its scale:

(1) We apply the word to the special physical *senses* of seeing, hearing, smell, taste, touch, etc., which precede conscious experience.

(2) We also use it to say that a man who can assemble the findings of his senses into a coherent picture has *sense*.

(3) We project this faculty or quality into the things we see or hear or study and say that *the sense* of that statement (cartoon, picture) is so and so.

It is useful to keep these different senses of *sense* in mind.

To Be Affected Is To Interpret

In this chapter, I shall use the words *interpret* and *interpretation* in a special way. No harm can be done, since the argument of this book does not anywhere depend upon a special interpretation of *interpretation*. Hereafter *interprets* will merely mean *is affected by;* interpretation will be the process of being changed or affected by something. The nature of the interpretation always depends upon the nature of the interpreter.

Looked at in this way, interpretation does not necessarily involve human beings or any living creature. A man looks out of the window, sees low black clouds covering the sky, and says it is going to rain. That is his interpretation of the weather signs. He looks at the thermometer in his room and then lights a fire. Half an hour later the thermometer has risen six degrees: that is the thermometer's interpretation of the changed climatic conditions. Instruments can tell falsehoods too. A Cambridgeshire farmer noticed his weatherglass set at "Fair" at a time when his barley had been deluged with rain for three days. (So he hung the glass on the outside wall of his pigsty and said, "Now, you old varmint, let's see if you'll believe it!")

If, for the present, we do not take too much for granted when we use the word *interpretation,* we stand a better chance of looking at the processes it customarily stands for and analyzing them in more detail. It is natural for us to suppose, unthinkingly, that we see, hear, and even understand things "in a flash," and that these are three simple and separate activities. But elementary physiology tells us that such processes are by no means instantaneous: it is our failure to carry over this knowledge that helps to prevent us from thinking sensibly about language and thought. Ambrose Bierce has a story in which a Southern planter named Farquhar is hanged from a bridge by Federal soldiers. He loses consciousness, recovers to find himself in the river, dives repeatedly from Northern bullets, and staggers across country toward his home. He is joyously hastening toward his wife when he feels a stunning blow at the back of his head. "Peyton Farquhar was dead; his body, with a broken neck, swung gently from side to side beneath the timbers of the Owl Creek Bridge." Such a story, in which the space of a few minutes is imaginatively elongated, sets a useful pattern for an attempt to contemplate sensory and thought processes in slow motion.

Seeing and hearing do take time. The resident of an undesecrated London used to be able to hear the chime of Big Ben from his wireless set and then later hear the same chime coming on its old-fashioned way through the window. Radio waves travel with the speed of light, while sound waves jog along at a more leisurely pace. (Of course, the physiological process of hearing from the radio takes as much time as hearing any other way, as soon as the stimuli become sound waves and reach the ear.) Even radio waves are not instantaneous: by the time they had traveled two hundred thousand miles, over a second would have elapsed. But, compared with this speed, the physiological processes of perception are almost at a standstill. It would take the human nerves more than eight seconds to carry their fastest messages over the distance of a kilometer, which is less than a mile.

When we see an object, at what stage in the journey between eying and realizing do we actually *see* it? The answer is that we see it all the time; every different stage in the perceptive journey between an object in the world and an individual who sees it and thinks about it represents a different meaning of the verb *see*. Similarly with *hear, smell,* and other such words. They have senses which arrange themselves in a hierarchy, like steps up a ladder. Before one can decide how such a word is being used on any particular occasion one must examine as thoroughly as possible the complete process concerned. For an understanding of *see, hear, perceive,* and *understand* we must consult physiology and psychology.

When we talk about an object being seen, or heard, or apprehended in any way, all we say is that this object causes certain happenings in us—chiefly in our nervous system. When I see something, my optic nerve and occipital region interpret my retina which interprets my lens which interprets the vibrations of light which interpret the object. And when I hear something, my brain interprets the auditory nerves which interpret the organ of Corti which interprets the stapes, incus, and malleus which interpret the eardrum which interprets the outer ear which interprets the vibrations of air which interpret the thing or happening which is "making the noise." In other words, what we see or hear—and I really should put the pronoun and the verbs in tiresome inverted commas—is some change in a sense organ. It is the sense organ that sees or hears the object. We should never say "I perceive a Thing" without remembering that our statement means: "I interpret Sense Organ, which interprets Thing"; or: "Thing changes Sense Organ which changes Me."

If there is only one chair to look at, do you and I, standing by different walls of a room, see the same chair?

This conundrum, though generally couched in more defensive language, has tortured many a thoughtful mind. It may be asked as a question about the nature of the universe, or about what we can know about the universe, or it may simply be a linguistical or logical question about how we are to use certain words. Whatever its scope, a sensible preliminary to the answering of this question is for one to give a physical description of the given situation and a semantic account of the words in the question. The situation could be illustrated by three drawings: of your view of the chair, my view, and the view of an outsider who sees all three of us; and these drawings could be described verbally in some such jargon as that I committed above—subject to correction by physiologists and physicists. Our linguistic analysis might well be focused on the word *same*. Each of us in the process of seeing "the chair" sees any number of chairs, one to represent each stage in the seeing process; and whether or not we see the *same* chair depends on which chair (at which stage of this perceptive process) each of us chooses to consider.

When we say we have interpreted something, then, we mean that our nervous system has registered the fact that some change has taken place in certain of our sense organs. We can generally find the objects which have affected our sense organs by checking with the evidence of other senses and other people. Our primary task is not to ponder philosophically about Truth or Perception or Knowledge or Beauty, but to do our best to reconstruct

the chains of happenings that link us with the world outside us.

Many errors and misunderstandings result from the
neglect of this primary verification. Writers on moral
and sociological subjects often stay in the clouds because
they despise such spadework. Many a literary critic, for
example, plunges into emotional abstractions while taking it for granted that everybody (himself included) of
course understands what happens when we read an essay
or a poem. Attempts to attack this fundamental problem
have been considered Philistine, even radical—and not
in the root sense of the word "radical"!

Dr. Richards attacks it in a chapter of his *Principles of
Literary Criticism.* In his analysis, the first thing that
happens when one reads a poem is that the reader's eye
is affected by the printed words, and this effect is quickly
followed by images, and then by the reader's thoughts
about the various sensations. Then come free, unasso-
ciated images, and after that the reader's thoughts about
the various things the poem talks about. At a further
stage his emotions are aroused by associations, rhythms,
and other factors; and thus slowly is built up the set of
attitudes which forms the reader's complete reaction to
the poem. This attempt to pave the way for a study of
the effects of poetry had a very mixed reception: there
are men of letters in all parts of the world who are still
offended at the insult cast upon the memory of "rare Ben
Jonson" by the suggestion that people have to have eyes
to read him with.

Context, Organism, Sign

Before taking up the interpretation of language, however, it is advisable to look at a simpler kind of Sign; though what is said in this chapter about signs is fully applicable to much speech, especially emotive speech.

A good thermometer interprets changes of temperature, as we have seen, but it has no memory. Our next concern is the interpretative process in organisms which remember and which do new things in the light of their own experiences. Such organisms have the power to interpret signs. The essential nature of a sign can be illustrated by a discussion of three familiar cases from the history of animal psychology.

Lloyd Morgan saw a chicken seize a black-and-yellow caterpillar and drop it again, evidently because it had a nasty taste. Some time later the same chicken was observed to encounter another caterpillar of the same color and refuse to have anything to do with it. Evidently there remained in the chicken's make-up some trace of the past experience as a whole—the picking up and the unpleasant taste. Its lesson was learned. We risk little in guessing that the chicken did not think the matter out logically; somehow it had been retuned, and the caterpillar looked repulsive. It was what in a human being we would call a prejudice.

Studies of animal learning have taught us much about the beginnings of the learning process. One experimenter put a cat in one box, and in sight of it, in another box, a fish. In the cat's box was a loop of string, so arranged that when the loop was pulled the door would open and the cat would be in a position to seek a peaceful settlement with the fish. The cat did a great deal of random milling about, but finally pulled the loop and got the fish. In later trials the cat pulled the string sooner, and finally got wise enough to go fairly quickly for the loop, although the loop's position in the box was changed. One would say that the cat's groping mind settled more and more definitely on the string as something pleasant.

In his famous conditioned reflex experiments, the Russian physiologist Pavlov placed his dog on a table, with braces slung from the roof of its box to keep it still. A tube connected the dog's cheek with a vessel ready to receive and measure the saliva secreted when the dog's mouth watered. A drum recorded the rate of the saliva's flow, and close at hand was an electric bell. Food was put before the dog; and its mouth watered dutifully. Pavlov then regularly rang the bell at the same time as the food was brought. After some repetitions, he rang the bell though no food appeared, and the saliva ran just as if the dog had seen the food. As far as the dog was concerned, the bell "meant" something good to eat.

These three animal stories provide an introduction to the Theory of Signs, which is fundamental to semantics. In each of these illustrations, a sign caught the animal's attention and reminded it of a past experience. Such signs, when they attract the notice of an organism, revive the sensations originally excited by a wider context. (By "context" here I mean a wider and more scattered experience, in which quite a number of things occurred; it will be necessary later to analyze this word more deeply, in its use in connection with symbols.) It is to be noted that each experience was interesting to the animal concerned, involving something very near to its heart, as we might say.

To consider in detail the essential characteristics of a sign, there are six points to be noted.

1. *A sign is an object similar to some object that has played a part in a previous experience.*

In semantics one generally does well to use "similar" and "like" in preference to "the same" and "identical." Even when we talk of things being "the same" and "identical" we are often speaking relatively, or metaphorically. Comparisons and parallels and archetypes and representative examples are the tools of the student of semantics; and if he forgets what kind of tools he is using he will not dig very far into the depths of Definition and Metaphor.

To consider our three illustrations: the objects acting as signs were in no case identical objects. It seems likely that the second caterpillar was only a very distant relative of the first. In the other two experiments, it may have been the same loop and the same bell all the time; but at different times the cat saw the string from different angles and there would doubtless be slight differences in the tone and intensity of the dog's bell. I should say here, too, that the word "object" is used above for the sake of concreteness: the actual sign is not the object itself, but the stimulus to the organism's senses which is *caused* by the object. In all three cases the stimuli would be similar but not the same.

All three objects are significant (that is, they are signs) because they were formerly parts of the black-and-yellow-seize-reject context, and of the loop-fish-eat context, and of the bell-food-eat context. No object can become a sign unless it makes at least two appearances.

2. *The sign is interpreted by an individual organism.*

As I have used the word "interpretation," anything that is changed by an object (or happening) *interprets* that object, but a sign can only be interpreted by a living organism. The process involved is well over the head of a stone or a thermometer. The organism has the capacity to take an object at more than its face value, to react to a sign as if that sign were the whole context. Reflection upon this point makes us realize that individuals differ enormously from one another, whether they are birds or human beings. Individual geese and ganders differ in far more than meets the eye.

A diagram may clarify this context-organism-sign relation, which in the next chapter will be compared and contrasted with the relation symbolized by the Triangle of Reference.

The context is the chicken's past experience, an effect of which remains in the organism. Note especially that the sign which "signifies" the context has no direct connection with that context. The two are connected only through the organism. The sign, *as a sign,* is purely artificial, and utterly dependent for its existence on the individual organism.

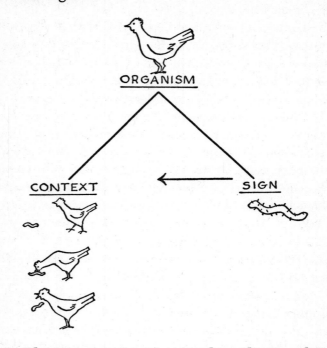

3. *The interpretation of a sign depends upon the organism's past experience.*

This seeming platitude is crucial. Not only does this particular interpretation depend on this particular experience (or a repetition of similar experiences), but the way the animal tackled this experience depended—I do not know to what extent—on past sign-situations, which in their turn were connected with earlier situations, and so on back to the animal's babyhood.

4. *The context interests the organism.*

In all three of our illustrations, the organism was interested in satisfying its hunger. Such urges as hunger, sex, and the desire to escape danger are obvious incentives to animal learning.

5. *The sign has a certain aggressiveness.*

The physical stimulus must have a certain energy, or intensity: it must be bright enough, or loud enough, or hard enough to excite the sense organs of the creature concerned. In a bad light the chicken might still seize a nasty caterpillar. It is probable, too, that the first caterpillar had subtle markings which could indicate its nonedibility more reliably than mere crude color, and that many black-and-yellow caterpillars are extremely eatable. It may be that the fowl did notice such markings in detail; but one cannot expect too much of a chicken.

6. *Signs are not permanent.*

Animals are less conservative about their signs than many people seem to be about their symbols. Pavlov found that when he stopped serving food the bell did not remain effective for very long. The dog's mouth soon ceased to expect a meal. No complete record of our cat's life history is available, but we would be ready to bet that he did not spend the rest of his life looking for loops.

These are all the characteristics of a sign that we need

to consider. In addition to applying them to the examples given above, it is helpful to reflect upon which of them are applicable to words; for example, to recently acquired words in one's vocabulary.

The matters discussed in this chapter are the subject of philosophical and linguistic controversy. Much of this controversy is waste motion, because little is known of what takes place in animal and human "interpretation"— that is why the word is used here with such modest assumptions. Some readers may object that this chapter has taken Causation or Causality for granted; but the answer to this objection would be that if *cause* (or *change* or *affect,* which are linked to *cause*) is taken for granted, the only assumption made is that as a word it undoubtedly exists. As such, it may be treated as a sign, possessing a sign's specified characteristics. This difficulty will, it is hoped, be further clarified by the next chapter, which is intended to throw more light upon the nature of referential words. The present chapter should be regarded as an endeavor to explain and illustrate the use of two terms essential to the technical vocabulary with which I shall describe linguistic situations. These two terms are *sign* and *context.* *Sign* is established, and *context* is clear enough for the present but will need further analysis in its connection with verbal communication. The final test of the adequacy of this chapter will be the success of these terms in performing their descriptive functions.

Chief Points

Seeing, hearing, and learning are complex processes. Science at the present time is able to give us knowledge in some detail of the different stages by which outside things get in touch with our minds. What our brain sees is not the thing we are "looking at," but the changes in our eyes of which that thing is the cause. If we keep this order of events in mind, we are in less danger of error.

Learning is an animal's (or a man's) reaction to Signs. A Sign is a part of an experience, that part which, coming back to the animal's attention, has the same effect as the complete experience had in the past.

Practice Exercises

I. Describe in terms of signs and contexts how a child might learn these words: label, affect, merry.

II. Describe in similar terms how a human being sees and recognizes a chair. What is the sign? Can such a sign be false?

4

SYMBOLS: *A WORD IS A SIGN OF THOUGHT*

Words are wise men's counters,—they do but reckon by them; but they are the money of fools.
THOMAS HOBBES, *Leviathan.*

A SYMBOL is a word used referentially. It is a special sort of sign: a word is always a sign, but not always a symbol. Let us verify the fact that words have the six characteristics attached to signs in the third chapter. Every time a certain word is spoken, written, or printed, it needs to resemble other sounds or marks closely enough to be recognizable as similar to them. Unless we are *thinking* about language, we are mostly only conscious of this fact when somebody writes a word badly, or mispronounces it. Secondly, a word can only be used by individual people, whose use and recognition of it depends upon their past experiences. Like the bell to which the dog responds, any word, whether acting as a symbol or not, must receive individual attention. Language may be compared with food. The French linguistic psychologist Delacroix has made an apt comparison in pointing out that food might be piled mountains high all over the world, but it would only become actual *food* by virtue of the chemical and physiological proc-

78

esses of digestion by individuals. Words might be stacked away in libraries everywhere; but we must never forget—it is the function of the Triangle of Reference to make it impossible for us to forget—that without human interpretation they cannot be symbols, or even signs. Interest on the part of the human being, and intensity in the sign or symbol, are also essential. We must be able to see or hear the word, and we need to be interested, before we can interpret it. And, lastly, things change, thoughts change, and words change. No student of semantics can for very long forget that words are not immutable.

Symbols, however, can be clearly distinguished from other signs. In a symbol-situation intentional communication occurs—there is a speaker as well as a listener, a writer as well as a reader. Looking at the diagram (page 81), one needs to remember the reciprocal nature of this process: the Triangle illustrated applies to the speaker, and the hearer's triangle would go the other way—from symbol to thought to referent. One of the chief things to be noted about symbols is that they imply a double consciousness on the part of speaker and listener. The speaker means to use symbols in order to communicate; the listener interprets the words *as* symbols.

A symbol differs from other signs in a second way. It is more abstract, and demands more discrimination from its interpreter. Even animals can understand words after a fashion—for instance, a cat easily gets accustomed to a word like "food" or "fish" or "salmon," and whenever it hears the word responds with some indication that it is looking for service. This does not mean that the cat interprets such a word exactly as we interpret the word "pig" in the Triangle below. The animal reacts to the memory of the whole context; but civilized man, exercising further discrimination, singles out objects, and to a greater degree leaves himself out of the picture. The interpreter of even the simplest symbol is on the third rung, as it were, of the interpretative ladder, the inanimate thermometer being on the first and the more malleable organism on the second. Man can, if he keeps his wits about him, climb indefinitely higher by sorting his symbols for different purposes: as when he calls a beetle an "insect," an "animal," or an "organism"; or measles a "disease" or a "handicap"; or grass-green "green" or a "color." Further details of such groupings and sortings—of generalizations, abstractions, Fictions, metaphors, and so on—will be considered in later chapters.

These, however, are relatively sophisticated problems. When our thinking goes wrong, it is nearly always because we have forgotten the simple truth that there is a difference between the name and the thing for which the name stands. The doll is not Cinderella herself. The label is not the overcoat. The signpost is not the city. The map is not the country. The book in the library is not the same as the happenings outside the library. The symbol is not the referent.

The Referent is the object referred to, the Thought is

the act of reference, and the Symbol is the name. Before any object can have a name, such a name must be in-

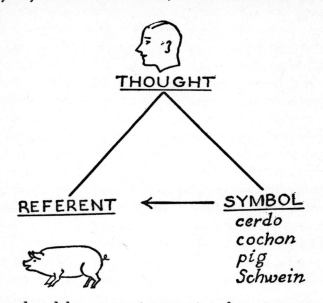

vented; and the constant intervention of man is necessary if the name is to keep alive.

Referent, Thought, Symbol

Imagine yourself to be looking at a signpost, near Schenectady, New York, say, on the road from Utica to Schenectady. The post has the word "Schenectady" plastered on its arm, which points east. Somewhere in that direction, at the end of the Dyke, over the Mohawk

River, embracing the bridge and Washington Avenue, lies the referent, your destination—Schenectady. Which three factors in this situation correspond with the three corners of the Triangle above?

It is useful to keep the signpost analogy in one's head, as a means of recalling and verifying the Triangle. This Triangle of Reference is the one detail in this book which needs to be remembered outright, by force if necessary. If the reader lost his book he could build up again for himself the subject matter of semantics, on the basis of the Triangle of Reference; for he would study as his subject matter words from his own individual experience, and the normal occasions on which he uses such words; and he could describe these matters in ordinary language. This is the best way to describe them. There are certain advantages in trying to present semantics in a purely technical terminology, but to my mind the more profitable course is to use a minimum of technical terms and strive to prepare the reader to see the referents of semantics (which in this case are ideas) whatever the symbols into which they are translated. If this book fulfills its purpose the reader will pursue his semantic interests in other volumes, especially in those to which this book makes reference. The Triangle will keep him oriented. What is more, reflection upon all that these triangular relationships imply cannot fail to renew his faith in education by, through, and for the democratic process, as well as giving him that respect for hard facts which is often supposed to be the privilege of totalitarians.

The subtitle of this chapter is taken from Jeremy Bentham's definition: "A word is a sign of thought." Bentham may have exaggerated; sometimes it is hard to believe that people are devoting any cerebral attention to what they are saying. One can safely say that a word is a sign; but this fact is no guarantee that it is a symbol. A symbol must have a referent. It often happens that a word is merely a sign to the hearer when there actually is a referent in the mind of the speaker. But sometimes even the speaker has no referent to keep his word up to standard. Are we always talking referentially when we speak of "the universal joint," or of "democracy"? We have already seen that "semantics" runs a similar danger. There are some words, too—of which the reader had best find his own examples from the terminologies of various myths and religions—which never did have any referents, though they have been used millions of times with the blithe assumption that they stand for something. Their use seems to follow the principle of the old Bible-punchers, who used to read on at the top of their voices till they came to a hard word, for which they would substitute "Jericho."

Word Magic

Men have always justly respected the usefulness of language; and they have always been prone to exaggerate its powers. It is only a step from talking as a means of organizing one's thoughts and activities to simply talking, and trusting the words to do the work. This is like giving orders without having a subordinate to carry them out. Words do so much with our help that we unconsciously expect them to do more than they can. And the consequence is that words act upon us like a magic spell. We are word-bedeviled.

Some old folk tales are very enlightening on this point. Folklore is a rich field for semantic study, and such research would give us a great deal of information about the awe-inspired attitude toward words which we inherit with them. The same stories crop up again and again in different parts of the world. It was natural for man to respect his words, which were helping him so rapidly to increase his control over his environment. It was inevitable that his words should get congealed in myths and religions, and later become a retarding influence.

The Grimm collection of German folk stories has an interesting example of word magic in a tale which was also long known in England and Scotland, under the respective names of Tom-Tit-Tot and Whippitystoorie. In the German version, a miller made the foolish boast that his daughter could spin straw into gold. The King ordered her to do it, under forfeit of her life. A mysterious little man came to her aid and for three nights spun straw into gold. Then she married the King. But she had promised the little man her first-born child. When the child was born, he came back to hold her to her pledge; but her grief so touched him that he offered to withdraw his claim if she could guess his name. She thought up every uncommon name she could but to no avail. Messengers scoured the kingdom, seeking outlandish names, and finally one of them discovered the truth. So came that triumphant hour when she was able to ask: "Can your name be RUMPELSTILTSKIN?"

There is a similar story of a cannibalistic troll who built a church for a farmer who had been set that task by his bishop. The troll claimed the farmer's child. The distracted father was lucky enough to hear a female troll hushing a baby to sleep with the soothing words:

> Tomorrow comes thy father Zi
> With Christian blood for thee.

Zi considered himself at a fatal disadvantage now that his name was known, and the farmer never saw him again.

Wherever he lives, man commits the fallacy of looking upon words as independent things, with powers and a life of their own. The Eskimo who has offended the white man's law will change his name and consider himself immune from further interference. If you swear at an Arab of the old school, he will fall flat on the ground, to let the words fly harmlessly over his head. The late Serenus Sammonicus offered the magic triangle based on the word "abracadabra" as a sovereign cure for fever, flux, and toothache. Until a few years ago, the names of beheaded Chinese were collected once every year, written on pieces of paper, and ceremoniously burned in a temple in Peiping; the deceased were not looked upon as quite dead until their names had been formally destroyed. And today we are all of us apt to yield without even taking the count when we are attacked by such words as Alma Mater, Americanism, Democracy, Honor, and Isolation. Coué, the autosuggestionist, who was word-bedeviled himself, would have done useful work if he had encouraged his disciples to chant every day: "The word is not the thing. The word is not the thing. The word . . ."

How Referential Language Works

The word "referential," introduced in the second chapter, now has a richer meaning if this discussion has been profitable. The person who efficiently interprets referential language remembers the three corners of the Triangle. He is conscious of himself as the apex, with the words on one hand and the objects on the other.

Let the reader make the experiment of reading the Encyclopaedia's description of insulin on page 50. He will need to consult books of reference to get a clearer idea of the referents of some unfamiliar symbols. Let him go into these symbols as deeply as he can, and then read slowly through the paragraph, trying to conjure up pictures of the actual things and people described—all of them—and making sketches and diagrams if he is not good at producing mental images. This sets a standard for the kind of reading which really puts the brain to work.

he Triangle of Reference enables one to judge any

book which is supposed to be informative. One should be able to translate its crucial paragraphs into different symbols, and to summarize and exemplify its chief points. The reader need not always sing small before a book which he has failed to understand. There will be times when he can parody Shakespeare's Cassius, and say:

> The fault, dear writer, is not in ourselves
> But in the book, that has no Referents.

Shifts and Changes of Meaning

Not for a day is any language static. It is like one's wardrobe—though with clothes one can make more drastic clean sweeps. Here a new hat appears, there a pair of shoes yield their place of honor to competitors, or there an old coat is forever discarded. It is the same with words. And some of them remain in circulation but change their meanings, like erstwhile ties now doing service as sashes.

It is not our province here to study the history of words and their meanings, nor to see how English words have cropped up and disappeared and changed their senses. It seems advisable, however, to give a few illustrations of the fact that there are three different tracks along which a word can change its direction. First of all, we must note that "change" itself has two clearly different senses. To change a coat may mean to make alterations in it or to discard it for another, and changing a word involves a similar ambiguity. So when we speak broadly of words having three different kinds of change—change of referent, change of thought, change of symbol—we must remember that "change" has this trick. The geographical term "Germany" today shows the first kind of change in its referent; a new *Victory* bearing the name of Nelson's famous old flagship serves as an example of a completely different referent, while the word "table" may have a piece of furniture or a list of statistical figures for its referent.

It is harder to distinguish change in the thought about the referent, partly because thoughts are less easy to discuss than words and things. We tend to add to the old thoughts, but not to discard them; much as we learn more about the physical composition of chairs than our grandfathers did, yet still tend, as they did, to sit on them. Our thought about the sun, for instance, is a richer conception than people had in the days of Joshua; but the sun still serves us as a lamp and as a clock, and it still awes us. Symbol changes, however, may be either partial or complete. The symbol may be contracted or otherwise altered, as when "cadet" became "cad," and "bus" resulted from "omnibus"; or the referent may acquire a totally different name, like the reconditioned submarine *Squalus* or those American destroyers which now fly the White Ensign of Great Britain.

Historically, the process of semantic change shuttles about among these three factors. But within our thoughts, our symbols every day follow far more subtle and complicated patterns of shift. The analysis of such patterns gives us new tools for controlling our thoughts. Seven of the most important patterns are: the shift along the Scale of Perception, the shifts from Process to Product and from Agent to Action, and the conditions or processes of Symbolization, Archetypation, Pregnancy, and Metaphor. We will briefly consider these seven here; other aspects of some of them will be treated in the chapters on Definition and Metaphor.

The Scale of Perception

This scale or hierarchy was discussed in the last chapter, in connection with symbols like "see" and "interpret." Could the reader describe the connection between the three different "views" in this sentence: "He took the view that they would get a better view of the view from the other side of the river"?

Process—Product

Such processes as building, cutting, education, learning, ruining, understanding, and wasting yield such products as buildings, cuts and cuttings, education, learning, ruins, understanding, and waste.

Agent—Action

The person or body of persons which cause a certain process or action to take place frequently share the name of that process. "Committee" and "government" are examples of this pattern, and so are "cook" and "guide."

Symbolization

This pattern has much in common with the process-product and the archetypation groups, but is important enough to be considered as a special case. It represents a process-product relationship in the same way that a symbol is the product of a thought. It occurs whenever a symbolized (usually a written) statement is treated as if it were the thoughts and processes which led up to the statement. Codified statements of court "laws" or of grammatical "rules" exemplify this shift. What *is* a law—a written statute, the process of passing it, or the operation of enforcing it? And what *is* grammar—a set of unwritten laws of thought, the rules in a grammar book, or the "authorities" who tell us when we go wrong? We tend unthinkingly to worship the written word.

Archetypation

This is the process of anchoring a word to some lucid and typical example of its use. The process of "advertisement" is archetyped by "an advertisement." Archetypation is especially useful in the study of language itself: it is the method of this book to exemplify by archetypes the mental processes involved when one uses symbols, referents, metaphors, Fictions, and so on.

The shift of "case" from A1 to A2 (page 35) seems to me another example of archetypation.

Pregnancy

Mr. John O'Hara described a certain playwright as someone "who writes one hell of a lot, but doesn't *write* very much." The second "write" illustrates the pregnant use of a word, in which there is an intensified focusing on what is taken to be the essence of the word's meaning. On page 35, the second sense of "body" (A2) exemplifies such focusing, in this case upon the idea of man without thought or emotion or life—a real or mere body. The arts of understatement would flourish if it were better understood that any word has this power to supercharge itself and produce what a gasoline-plus salesman would describe as that little bit extra. Cut down the description of one's neighbor as "a man who has a great deal of property" or "high personal qualities," and he becomes "a man of property," or "a man of quality." In the latter case, one may pay him the still higher compliment of focusing upon the central word, and simply saying that he is "a man."

Metaphor

Think of several parts of the body, and of how early in life we learned to lend their names to other things. A later chapter will examine why metaphor plays so strong a part in language. Though nouns often provide the handiest examples for discussion, other parts of speech are just as open to metaphorical use. Verbs, for example:

when we *give* advice, or *take* heed of it, we do not generally perform the physical operations of giving or taking. When a problem is *in* the mind, or *under* consideration, those spatial relationships are metaphorical. *Black* looks and *sharp* words are similarly removed from the kinds of sense experience which yield archetypes for these two adjectives.

Some sort of similarity is clearly the basis of all metaphor, but we must guard against linking our ideas of metaphor too tightly with the idea of visible resemblance. The similarity in a metaphor may be one of function, or of relative position, or of a score of other properties. Few "bottlenecks" look much like the neck (itself a metaphorical neck) of a bottle. The "bodies" of pages 35–36 in A4, A5, and A6 are all metaphorical, but the metaphors are of different kinds. How would the reader distinguish between them?

Neither metaphor (see Chapter 7), shift of meaning, nor definition (Chapter 6) can be considered in isolation, for some of their areas overlap. Often the question of how to classify a word depends on the point of view one adopts toward it; it can be looked at from different angles. Such ambiguity leads to no difficulties that a statement of the problem will not immediately solve. Take this line of reasoning.

> All men are mortal.
> Mrs. X is a woman.
> Therefore Mrs. X is not necessarily mortal.

Does "man" here mean "human being" or "male human being"? If the latter, there is a good argument for the conclusion; but if it means human beings in general it is connected to the more limited sense of "men" in the same whole-part relation which connects "poultry" with "cocks," and is similar to the connection between "rodents" and "rats." The fields of shift of meaning and definition merge here.

Or consider again our word "body." Which course does the reader prefer—to say that, without any suspicion of metaphorical usage, the word can be legitimately applied to:

1. All material objects?
2. Living creatures alone?
3. Only human beings?

The reader will see that upon his conception of the central sense of "body" depends his judgment on when that word is being used metaphorically. The semantically minded reader will be willing to see it as any one, or as all three simultaneously, and out of consideration for his fellow conversationalist he will take it or leave it alone as a metaphor. In case this seems a hairsplitting example, let us put "foot" in its place. Feet become paws as soon as we talk of animals, and the human term is frequently inappropriate. Many foreign languages are more touchy than English on this point: a Frenchman will not fail to take a reference to the foot (*pied*) of a bird as either jocular or metaphorical, because *pieds* belong to people.

The reader should refer back to this section when he comes to the chapter on Definition; and further links with shift of meaning will be established in Chapter 7, in which Metaphor, too, will be dealt with more fully.

False Symbols and Complex Referents

Symbols of model clarity, like our "pig," have two noteworthy properties. First, they are the equivalents of complete sentences. There is here no essential difference between words and sentences. To say the word "pig" is the same as saying "pigs exist" or "there are such things as pigs." Accompanied by the gesture of pointing, the utterance of the name represents direct symbolization, which is the fundamental form of definition: "That is a pig."

Second, words used on this level are either true statements or falsehoods. If one uses the word "pig" and points at something not a pig, one is lying. Similarly, if one uses "blilltum" as if it were the name of something, one is lying, because there is no such object. At least two objections to this standpoint may be anticipated. What about the symbols used in stories and novels and poems? Their referents do not necessarily exist; must they be classed as falsehoods? This complicated question can here be side-stepped with the remark that only the referential function of language is now under consideration. But how about hypotheses—how does semantics account for the way in which we all, scientist and workingman alike, venture to put forward words with a question mark, as suggestions, as a kind of guess? This vital matter, which will take us farther into the fields of metaphor and Fictions, is out of place with words of primitive lucidity like "pig." For present purposes we are talking in terms of white or black—truth or falsehood. Words like "unicorn" and "ghost" and "Loch Ness monster" are just plain lies.

Most falsehoods, however, are more complicated matters. Instead of being bad words, they may be bad combinations of good words. The referent of a whole chapter in a book is composed of a bundle of referents; and the chapter does not tell the truth unless it gives the reader a correct idea of how these referents really hang together. Most referents are complex, whether or not they can be represented by a single symbol. It makes no difference to a material referent whether it is symbolized by one word or by many, by one symbol or by the definition of that symbol. Different languages treat any given situation with varying degrees of conciseness. For instance, the French word *débarquons* means "let us get off the ship"; but the referent is not simplified by the fact that the French can cope with it in one symbol.

What applies to a phrase or a chapter applies also to whole speeches, articles, theses, and books. A classics professor is said once to have encouraged a student to write a thesis on the influence of Virgil on some obscure Latin poet. A year went by, and at the end of it the student had produced a whole pile of interesting material showing similarities between the two poets in style, expression, thought, and so on. But now it was discovered that the obscure poet had died before Virgil's time. The research work was a falsehood because the actual order of the referents had been confused.

The problem of muddled referents was clearly stated by the old preacher in the South who was explaining what he meant when he used the word "phenomenon." "If you see a cow, that's not a phenomenon. If you see a briar, that's not a phenomenon. And if you see a bird that's singing, that's not a phenomenon either. But if you see a cow sitting on a briar and singing like a bird, that, brethren, is a phenomenon."

As we proceed from rough general ideas to more precise knowledge of a thing, it changes in our minds from a simple to a complex referent. (We must not confuse change-of-thought with change-of-referent, nor forget that most of our referents are thoughts—about other referents.) We imagine things are simple until we get to know them; the mastery of any subject consists largely in seeing its complexities.

"Is It Good English?"

The big job of anybody communicating is to communicate—to get his meaning across, to make his hearer think of the same referents that he himself has in mind. "Grammar" is not nearly as important as we suppose.

It is curious that whenever we think about language, and especially about grammar, we tend to think of writing or print, and ignore those everyday situations which vitalize our linguistic powers. Take down in shorthand the conversation of ordinary people and you will get a record which reflects the subject-predicate formulations of the grammar books far less than one would expect.

Semantics is practical. The reader will quickly see what there is about the referents of the following words —which represent different grammatical parts of speech —that makes those words able to do the work of complete sentences. Go! Up! That! You! Again! Enough! Tomorrow! Contact! Tight! Quickly! They would cause many a grammarian's headache over whether they were verbs in the imperative mood, or articulated parts of complete but partly unarticulated sentences, or what; but few confusions of interpretation would arise over their use.

Even though a book on language professes to be merely descriptive, it becomes a linguistic influence on its own account if people read it. Subjects like grammar or phonetics are bound to be normative as well as descriptive. Grammar books must have some effect upon spoken English, though I doubt if they have much. What *does* make us prefer certain forms of speech to others? In the past, the big cities where all men met exerted the strongest influence. The great cities of Europe set standards of usage for the spoken Western languages. Today the world is the meeting place for English; we no longer imitate the English of any particular region; and we are getting to know too much about language to want to copy anyone slavishly.

Dr. Leonard Bloomfield once studied the speechways of a Menominee tribe, and found even there people who spoke "ungrammatically," although there was no writ-

ten grammar. Certain others were respected for their
skill with language, and imitated. In the present uncertain state of English grammar, we would probably do
well to consult on matters of usage only persons who are
obviously more skillful speakers or writers than ourselves;
and to consult grammarians only if we want to write a
grammar!

There are as many different sorts of grammar as there
are purposes for fixing linguistic rules. If English is one's
native tongue, the attempt to digest a grammar book is
apt to do more harm than good. Those who have not
learned the language in an English-speaking community
may need some artificial brand of "grammar" prepared
for foreign learners. But in either case, there is little to
learn by formal methods except the different forms of
the English pronouns and verbs—the cases and the tenses.
Even here uniformity is not quite complete; and, also,
such distinctions as that between "I saw him three times"
and "I have seen him three times" rest upon delicate
shades of meaning, and soon become semantic rather
than grammatical questions.

This seems the right moment to propose for English
syntax the "go-as-you-please" period that Sir Richard
Paget suggested for our spelling in his book on *Human
Speech*. We have run ahead of our grammarians, whose
science is still rooted in archaic Greek and Latin, and
who have panted to revise their views on "adjectives" to
keep up with *paper* napkins, *yes* men, *up-and-coming*
politicians, and *down* payments.

While in Peiping, I. A. Richards wrote a course of English syntax for Chinese students, beginning with sentence patterns that were models of clarity, and from them gradually working forward till all the elements of English syntax had been introduced. For home consumption, a straightforward grammar of this kind, showing the connections between all our common types of sentence with model sentences, and also discussing the forms, functions, and positions of words by comparison with the words of such pattern sentences, would harm no one. Grammar defeats its purposes when its classifications become too complex; it becomes an attempt by tinkering and renaming and patching to make watertight a system which by its nature can never be watertight. Diminishing returns set in. As far as the practical purposes of language are concerned, one would be more usefully occupied in working out a grammar for oneself. The sovereign test of any utterance lies in its success in communicating; and clarity (with economy, one aspect of clarity) must always be the speaker's chief concern. If he pursues these diligently, he will acquire correctness *en passant*.

However, there is a money side to this question. It appears that many people lose good jobs because they ignore the rules of accepted English usage. The worst offenders are those who once took a great deal of trouble to learn arbitrary rules and who do not see why their juniors should not take the same trouble. Those same juniors would do well to ascertain discreetly who the relevant authority is and "bone up" on him. Question-naires have shown Harvard businessmen and industrial-ists to be more snobbish about "grammar" than their fellows who became teachers or professors or writers. There is no harm in making up one's mind to follow usage, if one can discover what it is—as long as one does it with a grain of salt and takes occasional time off to reflect upon what a grammarian is, and where he gets his rules. "Grammar" interpreted on this level is a bread-and-butter question, not a subject for intellectual in-quiry.

C. K. Ogden considers that the various linguistic fields of grammar, philology, phonetics, rhetoric, semantics, should take their respective places in relation to a cen-tral subject which he would call Orthology. Words have not received their due. When we want to take up a special study, to learn a trade or pastime or science, we generally take some trouble to get acquainted with its terminology. We do not take its symbols for granted; we examine them, we make trials and errors, we experi-ment with the actual objects it is concerned with, its referents. It is an educational tragedy that up to now we have done no such thing with language, which should be the foundation subject of all subjects. The little child should be encouraged to see, hear, touch, smell, draw, and experiment with the referents of the words he uses —for which the words are only symbols. Childhood is the period when the relation between words, thoughts, and things, which the Triangle of Reference symbolizes, should be presented to our conscious minds. (Not in the form of dissertations on the Triangle itself, naturally!) As it is, we pick up our working vocabulary in a haphazard way, simply as so many signs, before we can read; perhaps we are given some drill in superficial aspects of some of our words, such as their conventional spelling; and by the time we are big enough to use the dictionary we are using it to look up the difference between "exposé" and "exposure"; or to find out whether the word we want is "exigent" or "exiguous." The child is seldom properly trained in the mastery of those primary words to which his more sophisticated vocabulary should be anchored.

There would be no need to make a fuss if all words were as simple as "pig," or if man had gone through the ages thinking fervently all the time about the Triangle of Reference. Our heritage is a language the bulk of whose words are ambiguous, and we need to know their ways if we are to steer them and not let them throw us. Their ambiguity ceases to be a danger and becomes an added resourcefulness when we realize the kinds of change they undergo. Semantics analyzes these changes and makes us conscious of them. The moral is not that a word should have only one referent, but that it should have only one referent at a time, and that when we shift its meaning we should realize what we are doing. Nor is there any need for continual self-consciousness about it; one can ordinarily use the words as they come, with the comforting feeling that when communication fails, or thoughts become confused, the semantic techniques can be called on. The basis of these techniques is the memory of the three corners of the Triangle.

How We Abuse Words

We have considered the errors which result when people regard a symbol as a cause rather than an effect. The chain goes the other way: Object caused Thought which caused Name. But man looked upon the name, and saw that it was good; and his verbal enthusiasm got the better of him. We have examples of the outcome in the infant who began his composition: "A rabbit is called a rabbit because he has long ears and a white tail and bunny fur"; and in the clergyman who declared with spirited benevolence: "The Divine is rightly so called."

Many examples of similar confusions on erudite levels are displayed in *The Meaning of Meaning*, which also quotes a witty educationist's definition of a "wousin." What is a wousin? It is a Negro climbing over a railfence with a melon under his arm while the moon is passing behind a cloud. The writer who provided the symbol for this rather complex referent remarked that "if this collocation of phenomena were of frequent occurrence, and if its happening were likely to affect the money market, we should have some such name as 'wousin' to denote it by. People would in time be disputing whether the existence of a wousin involved necessarily a railfence, and whether the term could be applied when a white man was similarly related to a stone wall."

A few years ago there was some vogue for the parlor game of "definitions." "What's a Bloogle?" "A Bloogle is a man who goes round with a torch to see if all the lights are out." "What's a Sneath?" "A Sneath is somebody who crawls about on his hands and knees to see how many of his centipedes have chilblains." "What's a Plimp?"—etc.

But some of them were funny. One is at a loss for good examples—no research student seems yet to have written a thesis on the subject, and for one reason or another those that stick in the mind are not very quotable.

Games like this help to show how accidental and arbitrary our words and definitions may be in their origins. Another game which is not unprofitable is that of defining the unspoken meanings of certain people when they use certain words. Our friends of political interests see "communists" and "fascists" and "fifth columnists" and "Trojan horses" and "warmongers" everywhere. What are the meanings of those words as they use them? There are educational institutions where "an incompetent teacher" is one whose intellectual outlook is unacceptable to the less literate of their governors. Parents and politicians are apt to regard a "good" child as one who has not sufficient curiosity to be enterprising. To some patrons of art, an aesthetic masterpiece is something which cost so many thousands of dollars. And so on. Living up to one's definitions involves courage and honesty as well as intelligence.

Chief Points

Words are Signs, and healthy words are Symbols. A symbol is an outstretched finger pointing to a Referent. Words have in great part been responsible for the increase in man's control over the things about him. But man is frequently overcome by his words. This is because not one of us is completely free from the error of looking on words as if they had a separate existence, with strange powers of acting by themselves. We are in far less danger of making this error if we keep clearly before our minds the order of the three parts of this chain: Referent—Thought—Symbol.

Practice Exercises

I. Draw a rough Triangle of Reference for the symbol *chair*. Compare it with the diagram on page 81—especially the base of your Triangle.

II. Make a short list of words which in your experience are very frequently misused.

III. Write down a few words which you yourself have trouble in using adequately.

IV. Start a file or a notebook in which to collect examples from your reading of different uses of the words in the two lists mentioned above; before long you will have examples of all their chief uses and be able to see which kinds of meaning-shift render them troublesome.

5

CONTEXTS: *A SYMBOL HAS MEANING ONLY IN ITS CONTEXT*

Anything has a cause, and the cause of anything is everything.

W. J. TURNER

A SYMBOL can have no meaning apart from its context. When we follow up this assertion we become involved in three peculiar difficulties. The most troublesome is that nobody will quarrel with it: almost every reader will be ready to accept it, will be fairly anxious to move on to something else. Yet, though we may accept it, it is doubtful whether we remain aware of it; that is the second difficulty. The third is that our intellectual acceptance is generally on the common-sense level; and here it is necessary to go deeper than that.

Thus, the tasks of this chapter are to bring home in a practical manner the importance of contexts, and also to explain why the recognition of their importance calls for scientific conviction rather than good intention. It has already been pointed out, in the second chapter, that an adequate description of an utterance must take into account, besides its referents, the attitudes of at least two people. And the technique of multiple definition which was explained in the Introduction merely represents an attempt to set forth the different sorts of context in which a given word can usefully occur. How did the reader manage to arrange the different senses of "case," on pages 34 and 35, unless by judging the word to have different contexts?

Contexts, however, do not always consist of words. We saw in the third chapter that a context is a bundle of things which happen together. Its different factors may be specified—for example: hunger, caterpillar color, caterpillar shape, nasty taste—but to any list we make we must add the factor x, to stand for the particular relationships which bind the bundle together into a system. There is a causal connection between the various factors in a context, or, at least, the organism behaves as if there were, and thereby, so far as the sign-situation is concerned, causes the causation. On future occasions, the recurrence of some or even one of the factors may bring back the "memory" of the whole experience: the color *means* the other things. As Dr. Richards expresses it in *The Philosophy of Rhetoric:* "What a sign or word means is the missing parts of the context." So any word we utter never means itself, but all the other relevant factors, in the relevant contexts in which it has previously occurred!

Contexts at Work

The importance of contexts can easily be established, if the reader will co-operate in one or two experiments.

The first calls for "referential reading" of the kind he was asked to do with the paragraph on Insulin, although this time the material is less technical and notes and diagrams will not be necessary. It is a story from Herodotus, which is to be read closely and, for purposes of the experiment, considered as historical fact.

Introduction

A boastful king had one courtier who was his great friend, and to whom he confided his most delicate secrets. One of his favorite topics was the beauty of his queen, a lady of unparalleled modesty. The courtier politely agreed with his royal master's eulogies, but never with enough enthusiasm to satisfy the monarch.

"He must see for himself," the king decided. So he insisted upon his friend's hiding behind a door in the corner of the royal bedchamber. The courtier, not liking the idea, at last very grudgingly obeyed; and the queen saw him when he was slinking from the bedroom.

She was outraged. Next day she sent for the courtier and gave him the choice of two courses. Either he must kill the king, or he must die himself. She would never tolerate her present disgrace. What was the courtier's decision?

This story has two different endings. Read the first, which follows immediately.

First Version

The bewildered courtier begged her not to bind him to so terrible a choice. But since he could not persuade her, and he realized that he had either to kill or be killed, he considered it more advisable to remain alive. "Your Majesty," quoth he, "since you pitilessly compel me to take the life of my king, let me hear the manner in which we shall set upon him." "Of a truth," replied she, "our treason shall be performed on the very spot where he shamed me. The assault shall be given when he is asleep." The wretched courtier, unable to escape this predicament, obliged to kill or to be killed, went with the queen to her room, and stood secretly in the corner; and afterwards emerged and assassinated the king, thus winning his spouse and his kingdom.

Now read again the Introduction, *not* the First Version, and then jump to the second ending, reading it carefully with a view to describing the difference between the two endings.

Second Version

The dumfounded gentleman entreated her not to hold him to such a hard condition. Yet as all his arguments were in vain, and he saw that it was necessary to slay or be slain, he deemed it better to live himself. "My Lady," said he, "as you force me without mercy to become guilty of the blood of my sovereign, tell me by what means the deed must be accomplished." "In sooth," she answered, "the treachery must be effected in that same place in which he betrayed me. The attack must be made while he is sleeping." The poor gentleman, placed in this dreadful dilemma of having to slay or be slain, followed his lady to her chamber and hid behind the door; whence later he came out and murdered his sovereign, and gained both his lady and his crown.

When we come to discussing the difference between the two endings, there is little to discuss. They are the same. The same pictures or events or ideas came to the reader's mind in both cases—if he really read them referentially, remembering that words are not things and using his thoughts to build up pictures of the referents. If you will not agree that the two referents ("things referred to") are the same, how much do they differ—by what percentage, if we can make a rough estimate in numbers? Fifty per cent? No. Ten per cent? Probably not. But let us be generous and say 15 per cent. The referents of the two versions differ by not more than 15 per cent.

But how does it happen that the difference is so small? There is a huge difference between the symbols used in the two versions. Altogether, 160 different words are used; and only 22 of them are used for both versions of the ending. (According to my count they are: a, and, be, he, her, him, his, in, is, it, me, my, not, of, or, she, that, the, this, to, which, you. Take a passing look at these highly interesting words—they will be referred to in a later chapter.) Twenty-two is not a very high proportion of 160—it is well under 15 per cent. Why is there not an 85 per cent difference between the two sets of referents?

Our linguistic conscience rebels against such a statistical approach: the problem is one of contexts rather than of percentages. We can express it simply by supposing that the two passages used respectively symbols

A, B, C and C, D, E to stand for the same context: abcdex; this is a vast oversimplification of the complexities, but it gives the right idea.

The context of anything is the frame or field or setting in which it exists. The idea is familiar enough to anyone who has used words like "environment," "milieu," or "system."

Three Types of Contexts

In semantics there are three types of contexts: *symbol contexts, psychological contexts,* and *physical contexts.* In normal speech we tend to take it for granted that a context is always a symbol context. Probably we think of questions on school examination papers:

" 'Whose grave's this, Sirrah?'

'Mine, sir.'

'I think it be thine indeed, for thou liest in't.'

Explain these words with reference to their context."

Sometimes the essential context of a group of words consists of other words; but sometimes it does not. The film critic of a newspaper dislikes a picture, and writes in his review that it is "definitely a good picture from which to stay away." Then the theater may advertise: " 'HOT SPOTS is definitely a good picture' (*Daily Post*)." Thus the original review is falsified by having seven words plucked out of their context.

These are examples of symbol contexts. But let us take an everyday situation (in a peacetime world). An Australian family deeply interested in cricket is following a series of test matches, of which so far Australia and England have won two each. Father comes in one evening and announces that "Bradman has broken a finger." The whole family knows that these words "mean" far more than their five words say. Their meaning depends upon a context which is not a verbal one but a context of happenings in which Don Bradman has played an important part, and a context of hopes and calculations and fears in the minds of the members of this Australian family.

In our experiment the context consists mainly of the introductory paragraphs. Without this context, each version would have to be more detailed and explicit, and the two versions might have to use more words in common. As it is, the context gives information which is taken for granted. Half the battle in understanding what anybody is saying consists in making a mental note of the things he is taking for granted. Three quarters of our conversation would sound "haywire" if it were considered apart from its context. One remembers from 1930 the placards—SHE'S THERE!—of an evening newspaper which were rushed along the London streets during the time when everybody was wondering whether the aviatress Amy Johnson would get to Australia.

In ordinary life, a context is generally something very different from a written introductory paragraph. A context is what makes one able to tell a story to a friend (who, in our common-sense idiom, "talks the same language") in fewer words than one could to a stranger.

We never "tell all." Indeed, the best speaker or writer is often the man who can leave most out and get a few words to do a lot of work. Also, no word is indispensable. For any particular job any word can be passed up and its whole function performed by another word, or other words, and it never will be missed. This assertion will be elaborated upon in the next chapter, but the mere fact that there can be such a thing as a dictionary is sufficient proof of its truth.

The reader can try another experiment, if he will get a piece of paper and on it jot down a—— b—— c—— twice. Reading through the paragraph which follows, his first task is to write down three times one word which makes sense in all three of the blanks.

"Dr. Benson was already in the workroom, and had sat down to wait on a toolbox, with his back against the —— of a high bench. He felt relieved when he saw, limping through the door, relying heavily on the —— of his chauffeur, the old gentleman to whose —— most of the town's charities owed their existence."

Secondly, use three different words.

If the reader did this little test and feels satisfied with his results, the chances are that he got the right words; but the point is that, as far as effective communication is concerned, no one word here is *the* right word because there is no such thing. One word does the job as well as the other. Any preference we may happen to show is due to extra intentions which restrict our choices. Here, for example, we might want to write with a pleasing literary style, and avoid repeating the same word—or, on the other hand, we might want to show some of the possibilities of the word "support." As far as simply "referring" to the referent is concerned, the choice is fifty-fifty. Indeed, as we see, the context here is strong enough to permit most of us to catch on with the use of no words at all.

In semantics, besides accepting the importance of contexts, we must have definite ideas about their nature. Nothing much is settled by burbling: "Of course, one always has to consider the context." The word should be used carefully, because, as we have seen, there are three distinct types of context.

One way of clarifying the distinction is for the reader to think of the Triangle of Reference. At the foot of the symbol leg let us picture a book—a geography textbook of Australia, let us say. This book represents a symbol context. At the top of the Triangle is the head of a student, wearing a mortarboard. If he is a Cambridge (England) undergraduate, the tassel will be cut level so that its end does not flop over the flat edge; but this is not a fact on which our argument depends. The diagram stands for the student's thoughts about Australia; in general terms, for a psychological context.

Finally, at the referent corner, is a map of Australia, a rather kidney-shaped mass of land which looks as if a great giant had chopped out the Gulf of Carpentaria from its top with a rectangular spade, and as if the Great

Australian Bight at the bottom had been made by the teeth of a still larger giant. This diagram represents all the objective facts about Australia, known and unknown. It is a physical context. The three types of context to be distinguished, as we have shown, are physical, psychological, and symbolic.

There is no need to stop at Australia—we can widen our range to the limit. Each of us has his own machinery of words and his own ways of manipulating it. All the words you or I have ever met can be considered as a network, very intricately interconnected, which has an existence apart from the networks of other people. When we talk or write, we share that bit of our network with those who hear or read us; otherwise there could be no such thing as communication. But we ought to feel sobered when we consider the differences between our individual networks.

There are as many different symbol contexts as there are different persons in the world: probably at present about two thousand millions of existing symbol contexts.

A similar story can be told of our thoughts. Every individual puts together his experiences with words and his experiences with objects and weaves them into an outlook, a way of thinking—what the Germans call a *Weltanschauung*. There are two thousand millions of different psychological contexts in the world.

Finally, there is the total context of existing things. This embraces all referents, whether symbolized or not, whether known or unknown. All animals, vegetables, and minerals, biology's organs in their organisms, literature's writers in their milieus, sociology's lawbreakers in their environments—all these are parts of the physical world, different sections of which are studied by the different sciences.

The world has only one physical context.

For us, the practical problem is to remember which of these three contexts we are thinking about. The discussion immediately above has inflated all three beyond their customary size: the contexts we are normally interested in are bits of contexts, and it is to such bits that the word will hereafter be applied again.

We must constantly bear in mind the way symbol, psychological, and physical contexts overlap one another. One cannot know a word without having thought about it; thus, all of our symbols are parts of psychological contexts. In the physical world, every referent known to us or anyone else has contributed to a psychological context—in most cases, to thousands of psychological contexts. So psychological contexts link up too with physical contexts; or, to put it another way, psychological and physical contexts combine to form wider physical contexts—for all contexts are contained within physical contexts.

Suppose for some reason we had to write an account, giving all the facts, of how Mr. Wells wrote his *Outline of History*. We might, if we were stupid enough, decide to do three neat little essays: on Mr. Wells's words, Mr. Wells's mind, and Mr. Wells's referents. But our real task would be to consider the interconnections between those three types of context. The words he uses have a history of their own, which thousands of books have not finished telling. The history of how Mr. Wells got to know all the words he used in his *Outline* would be a long and complicated story, involving his experiences with thoughts and things as well as with words. Even chickens and caterpillars carry wherever they go traces from past contexts with which they have been concerned; how much more complex must such traces be in a Mr. Wells. They affect his thoughts as well as his words, so that his thoughts are results of all his past contacts with words, thoughts, and things.

As for the referents of his book, those are linked up in past contexts with workers and fighters and discoverers of old. Writers before him had dealt with these facts, interpreting and misinterpreting them. Mr. Wells's authorities and sources, oral and written, would all need to be brought into our account.

So the complete story of Mr. Wells and his book becomes a universal history, only a few strands of which are hinted at in the *Outline* itself.

The Receding Referent

One last peculiarity, inherent in the way we think, causes trouble when we concentrate our attention on a physical context or on a referent. When we try to find a physical context, it eludes us. This chapter has spoken of a physical context as if it were so much matter. But is it? Really, a physical context is composed only of the *relevant* physical factors, and who or what decides what is relevant but the organism?

Let us start afresh for the moment, and make sure we can clearly see the difference between:

1. The physical context that *is there* (*sub specie aeternitatis,* as Spinoza put it).

2. Those parts of the physical context (1) that are noticed by the organism.

3. The psychological context.

Considering the properties that make up a context, the physical context in any given example will be (2). But we have to speak of (2) as if it were (1); otherwise it merges into (3)!

Referents behave in the same way; we can never catch them by sidling after them inch by inch. Achilles may have felt certain that he could catch a tortoise, but with mathematics the way it was in his day he was totally powerless to prove it. So our linguistic machinery balks at the task of proving that the most physical of referents "exists." I look across the room and see a chair, and formulate this situation in terms of the Triangle of Reference: "chair," symbol; my chair, thought; the chair, referent. But as soon as I think of the chair it becomes my chair, and the chair behind it becomes mine when I think of that, and so does the one behind that. All the time, *the* chair steadily recedes. This is like swimming after one's own ripples.

For most purposes, the last section of this chapter is

not relevant, and need not be taken into account; but the only weapon against this difficulty is knowledge of it.

Chief Points

The Context of anything is the field in which it has its place. There are three different sorts of contexts: of words, thoughts, and things; but every context has connections with other sorts.

When using language, we never give all the details of the things we are talking about. Our words are dependent for their full effect upon our hearer's knowledge of the context. So it is clear that there is no such thing as "*the* right word," or "*the* right way" of making a certain statement.

Practice Exercises

I. Provide contexts for the following statements by writing down some (say two to five) of the assumptions they seem to be making.

1. We cannot trust reason.
2. Vote for Jones and a full dinner pail.
3. I strove with none, for none was worth my strife (W. S. Landor).
4. When capitalism arose, agriculture was in the state of feudalism (A. Leontiev).
5. When it declares war, a nation subjects itself to the very evils it thinks it is fighting.

6. We learn from history that we do not learn from history.

7. Women have failed to attain eminence because they have been denied the advantages of education enjoyed by males.

8. Although inferior to the Caucasians, the Oriental peoples are not as inferior as either the Negro or the Indian.

9. Wherever fleas are, they jump onto white colors. This instinct was given them in order that we might more conveniently catch them (Bernardin de Saint-Pierre).

10. A man who has found his place in the social whole has all the faith man can hope to have and all the morality he needs (Harvey Fergusson).

11. It is not knowledge that generates good ideas: you can be a walking encyclopedia and make only $20 a week (an advertisement).

12. Women ought not to be licensed as air pilots. Scientific tests have shown that on the whole women are not such good automobile operators as men; and it has also been proved that the best car drivers make the best pilots.

13. When we say that the universe exists objectively now, what we say also is that the past experience of mankind, as it is summated in the speech, writings, libraries, and institutions of modern society with all our sharpened thinking, also exist objectively now.

To think truly about the universe, then, we must bring to bear on the problem, not merely our direct personal experience, but all that vast experience of the race (H. Levy).

II. Get someone else to do this, and pool your findings.

6

DEFINITION: *TWENTY-FIVE DEFINITION ROUTES*

> *Mr. Jorrocks felt confident. "Look out of the vinder, James, and see wot'un a night it is," said he to Pigg. James staggered up, and after a momentary grope about the room—for they were sitting without candles—exclaimed, "Hellish dark and smells of cheese!" "Smells o' cheese!" repeated Mr. Jorrocks, looking round in astonishment, "smells o' cheese!— vy, man, you've got your nob i' the cupboard—this be the vinder."*
>
> SURTEES, *Handley Cross or Mr. Jorrocks's Hunt.*

LOGICIANS do not agree on the definition of "definition." Professor L. Susan Stebbing, in *A Modern Introduction to Logic,* will not accept exemplification, or definition by similarity ("a sonnet is a poem like Keats's poem on Chapman's *Homer,* or that poem of Wordsworth's on *Westminster Bridge*") as being definition at all. Nor does this scholar accept simple naming ("Mr. Robinson is that man I am pointing at") or definition by translation (*"Tapferkeit* means *courage"* is Miss Stebbing's example) as definitions in her sense of that term. Other logicians disagree on one or other of these points.

In this chapter, however, we are interested in all such processes of clarification or explanation, in the definitions of the scientist or the logician, but equally in definition

as used by the man who has seldom even heard the word.
("What's all this about 'one man, one vote'?" asked the
Nottingham miner. "Why, one bloody man, one bloody
vote," Bill replied. "Well, why the 'ell can't they say
so?")

Some writers and teachers, trying to widen the scope
of definition, have set up a division between logical definition and psychological definition, but this dichotomy
is not altogether fortunate. All of the logician's defining
activities can be accounted for under one or other of the
headings set forth in this chapter, but "definition" is not
here used in its logical sense only. As usual, the reader
is asked to work out his own definition of the word which
serves as the focal point of discussion.

Analysis of a Journey

Anyone who wants to get from Grand Central Station in New York to the City Hall may simply take a taxi.
If he does this, he is of no use to us as an example. But
an economical man will travel there more cheaply, even
if he has to ask his way. He can take the IRT or BMT
subway, or he may go by the Third Avenue Elevated, or
even by a Broadway bus. There are a vast number of
different ways and combinations of ways of getting from
the one place to the other. But there are only a few different *kinds* of ways; it would be quite easy to draw up a list
of them. Military experts draw up similar lists when they
arrange to blockade an enemy country. Definition is
very much like the process of telling someone how to

get from Grand Central to the City Hall: it is simply the process of explaining the way from one word to another. In both cases there are three factors:

<blockquote>
One, the starting point
Two, the route
Three, the destination
</blockquote>

The explainer starts with the destination, then goes to the starting point, then to the route, and so back to the destination.

We had better deal now with a little quibble. In definition, do we define the referent or the symbol? Do we define an actual dog, or democracy itself, or merely define the symbols "dog," "democracy"? Probably the reader feels that he does define the actual animal, while with democracy he merely substitutes one (or more) symbol for another. Let us state the question in a more general way. Taking definition as the process of substituting S for S_1 we see that

<blockquote>
S_1 stands for r
S_2 stands for r
</blockquote>

Clearly S_2 throws light on the total situation, thus defining the interrelations of three things, including itself. We must *not* from pressure of habit go on to conclude that $S_1 = S_2$!

All one has to do, in order to explain a word to somebody, is to find, as a starting point, a symbol whose referent you and he can both agree on, and then use a "definition route" which he can follow. If, like James Pigg, you choose a quite inappropriate route, no won-

der the results are mysterious! There are not many different definition routes—the number of general ideas we
use to explain or define some term to somebody else is
surprisingly limited.

It is well to emphasize that in making a list of these
routes one is merely tackling a technical linguistic job.
We want to find thought-tracks which our experience
tells us we can think about, and symbolize, apparently
without irreparable confusion. We steer a course between the essences and ultimates of philosophy and
the direct-and-indirect objects and objective-genitives
of grammar. We need a list which will be sufficiently detailed to be manipulable and not so ramified as to lose
itself in a bookful of detail. Much will have been accomplished if this list proves workable—and the criterion of
its success rests upon whether the reader understands
the description of it, and whether he can use the routes
to analyze all the definitions he comes across, in the dictionary or elsewhere.

By defining, in the sense of limiting, their task, Ogden
and Richards have improved upon their predecessors.
Aristotle dug deeply into many parts of the problem,
especially in his *Metaphysics,* in which, besides dealing
formally with logical definition, he stated the more general problem in his four "causes"—material, formal, efficient, final.

Logicians have been attacking certain areas of the
problem ever since; but more relevant here are such
efforts as those of Amarasimha, who worked out a vo-

cabulary of the Sanskrit language some time before the Battle of Hastings. This was a list of Sanskrit words arranged in sections under the headings of different general ideas, the first section comprehending "Heaven, Gods, Demons, Fire, Air, Velocity, Eternity, Much." However, "a more logical order pervades the sections relating to natural objects," wrote Roget, "such as Seas, Earth, Towns, Plants and Animals, which form separate classes; exhibiting a remarkable effort at analysis at so remote a period of Indian literature." Bishop Wilkins's "scheme of analysis of the things or notions to which names were to be assigned" was an attempt to formulate a system of abstract symbols which would be a truly "philosophical language" and serve as a universal tongue; but, alas, not even kings were philosophers enough to understand it. In his *Thesaurus*, first published in 1852, Peter Mark Roget arranged the words of the English language, "according to the ideas which they express," under the six classes of Abstract Relations, Space, Matter, Intellect, Volition, Affections; and his labors were successful to the extent that many of us still turn to adaptations of his work when we are at loss for a word.

Theoretically, one can see some of the possibilities of a successful theory of definition, but how much does it matter practically? If this chapter does its work properly, it should have two important results for the reader. It will teach him the how and the why of an operation he has always performed automatically, and it will have the practical outcome of making him more systematic and more resourceful in explaining matters to other people, which is one of the most important things any human being ever has to do. When one is acquainted with the principles of definition one chooses the common ground—a familiar starting point—more carefully, and wastes less time in finding the easiest roads to the desired destination. Even a faulty list of such roads is better than none, and is a first step toward finding a satisfactory list.

The kind of route under discussion may be illustrated with reference to a well-known breed of dog. This is the German "police dog," used for police purposes, which is also called an "Alsatian" since it originally came from Alsace, in Eastern France, and in Europe is sometimes called a "wolfhound" because it looks very much like a wolf. Here we have an idea of a certain referent—a particular brand of dog—which is arrived at along three different routes, all starting at the general idea of "a dog." The three routes here used are those of Use, Place of Origin, and Similarity. There is room for dispute about this last: if we looked deeper we might decide to substitute Causation for Similarity, because the dog probably looks that way on account of a partly wolfish ancestry. (Or we could decide that both these routes are involved—many defining-words that look simple use two or three or more of the definition routes.)

When we say that we use a limited number of routes in the process of definition, we merely say that we link up specific terms with more general (or more familiar) ones by using a small number of connections. All these connections could be grouped under the five headings of similarity relations, part and whole relations, causal relations, space relations, and time relations. Many readers will think that even these five should be telescoped into two or three, but there are theoretical as well as practical reasons for refusing to give too much thought here to these large problems. Besides getting us into philosophy, which we must avoid for this purpose, such generalizations run us into the risk of jellying our outlook, at a time when man's scientific knowledge is not at the "jellable" stage. Our best bet is to make a minute analysis and keep open the questions over which men of good will are amicably wrangling. Readers with differing points of view may do some telescoping of their own if they care to. My task is to get the reader's support for the principle of attempting this task, however he may argue with details in its performance.

For let me emphasize that every definition is unique. One takes a symbol which happens to become important in a discussion, and defines it by expanding it, by using other symbols to throw light on the way one is using it. The question of when to stop is always a new problem and always a practical one. If you stop too soon, you are in for trouble; if you go on too long, you become a bore. (A country editor, after a visit from a very angry retired warrior, rushed to the desk of one of the cubs and demanded: "What do you mean by this?" The reporter followed his boss's finger and read, "Among the prettiest young ladies present at the garden party was Colonel Bloodstone." He looked up and said quite firmly, "Well, that's where he was." A knowledge of the theory of definition would have taught him to expand "among" by explaining that his report had used it in the sense of "in the midst of"—not "one of.")

Twenty-five Definition Routes

The trouble about all this kind of stuff is that when tabulated and codified it seems intolerably abstract, though in actual fact definition is a most practical operation. So throughout the discussion of the following list of definition routes—which covers all the different ways of expanding a symbol—to explain the way the author is using it gaps have been left for the reader to supply whatever word or words make the best sense to him. In doing this, the reader cannot help following the road which is being discussed. The proof of the road is in the journey. If any particular place gives trouble, this may be a sign that the reader's thinking is clogged a little along this line. (Though it is hard to make all examples equally lucid and the trouble may be the author's fault.)

This is the list of definition routes.

Route 1. *This is it.*

DIRECT SYMBOLIZATION
Many an argument has to be rooted to a concrete situa-

tion before it can branch out successfully. Conversation with foreigners proves this most dramatically; but all the time we do it more than we realize. "What I call my hand is . . ." and we touch it. "The window is . . ." and we point to it. In the last resort, we may have to take the stranger to his station, and point out the City Hall.

Route 2. *It is similar to this.*

SIMILARITY
You may draw the thing you are trying to describe, or you may express its similarity to something familiar to your hearer. "A bat is a quadruped — a mouse, with membranous wings."

Route 3. *Its name may be translated by this word.*

TRANSLATION
A person who speaks a different dialect, or a foreign language, or has different interests, may know a lot about the referent, but may not recognize the symbol. "A stout fellow is a swell guy." "A mammal is an ——." "A gob-stopper is a marshmallow." "A concierge is ——."

Route 4. *It is contained in this.*

PART AND WHOLE
"A foot is —— a leg." "A company is —— an infantry regiment."

Route 5. *It contains this.*

WHOLE AND PART
"A series is a number of —— of one kind, following one another in order."
"A committee is a —— — —— appointed or elected to perform some function."

Route 6. *It is the opposite of this.*

OPPOSITION BY CUT
"Left is —— —— right."
"White is —— —— black."

Route 7. *It is at the opposite end of a scale from this.*

OPPOSITION BY SCALE
Two opposition headings are necessary: one stands opposite one's mirror in a different sense of "opposite" from the way the top of a flagpole is opposite to its base. "Directly opposite" and "at the opposite end of" are two different relationships, just as opposite walls do not show the same kind of opposition as do the opposite ends of a carpet. The walls are cut apart by the intervening floor; while it is carpet, carpet, all the way, from one end to the other. "The top is —— —— the bottom." "—— —— of boiling water is —— water."

Route 8. *It resides in this place.*

PLACE: WHERE
"An occupant is a person —— —— a certain place." "A Siamese is a person —— —— —— the country of Siam."

Route 9. *It comes from this place.*

P L A C E : W H E N C E
"Virginia tobacco —— —— Virginia, and Siamese cats from Siam."
The distinction is clear enough, but it is not easy to find for nine examples which might not also apply to eight.

Route 10. *It has this age.*

A G E
"A centenarian is — —— —— —— ——." "A parr is a —— salmon."

Route 11. *It lived in this period.*

P E R I O D
"Medieval things belong to — —— ——." "The Augustan period in Latin literature occurred — — —— of Augustus Caesar."

Route 12. *It has this shape.*

F O R M
"A triangle is a rod of polished steel bent —— —— ——, which is sounded by being struck with a steel rod."
"Siamese twins are twins who are —— — each other."
"A brachycephalic is a person with a —— ——, the breadth of whose skull is at least four fifths of its length."

Route 13. *It has this size.*

SIZE
"A giant is a —— person." "A microbe is a —— living being."

Route 14. *It has such and such a quality, characteristic or property to this extent.*

DEGREE
"A mule is an animal which is —— horse and —— donkey." "A saturated solution is one in which there is only just —— of the dissolving agent — —— all of the substance." "A mulatto is a person whose ancestry is —— Negro, and —— white."

Route 15. *It is made of this material.*

SUBSTANCE
"A can is a —— vessel, in which fruit, fish, etc., are sealed up airtightly for preservation."

Route 16. *Its material is in this condition.*

STATE
"A corpse is — —— — of a man." "A feudal society was based on the relation of lord and vassal arising out of the holding of lands in feud."

Route 17. *It causes this emotional reaction in a human being.*

CAUSATION: EMOTIVE
"A darling is someone ——." "A cur is a —— dog." "A

scoundrel is a person ——." "A friend is ——." Emotive definitions of this kind can be very tricky, as we saw in an earlier chapter. But though emotive language must not be used for referential purposes, it would be most unscientific to try to ignore its existence.

Route 18. *It has this effect on the human mind.*

CAUSATION: MENTAL

"A surprise is an event for which one —— —— ——." "A masterpiece is a piece of work — —— ——." To what extent is it possible to distinguish between mental and emotive causation in actual communication? As was seen in Chapter Two, we can easily see the difference between extreme examples of the two types. But, especially in ethics, aesthetics, and philosophy, many definitions and utterances use Routes 17 and 18 together.

Route 19. *It has this effect on the human senses.*

CAUSATION: SENSORY

The important thing to remember here is that a red curtain is a curtain which gives a "red" sensation to our eyes; a rough brick is a rough-sensation brick; bitter quinine is bitter-sensation quinine; and so on. No philosophy is involved here—I am not saying that bricks and curtains and quinine do not exist. The sole point here is that their characteristics of color, taste, smell, touch, and the like are specifically named *for* their effects on the senses. In general, when we want to be objective we leave out the human being, but obviously here that is just what we cannot do; it would be like emptying a flood from a deluge and expecting to find something left. This route could be subdivided and the sensations classified according to whether our muscles are affected or our skin, our taste buds, our olfactory cells, our auditory nerves, or the cells of our retinas.

"A ruby is a —— precious stone." "Quinine is an alkaloid, —— in taste, which is found especially in cinchona bark." "A shout is a —— cry." "A file is a metal instrument with a —— face."

Route 20. *It has this physical effect.*

CAUSATION: PHYSICAL

We could split up all these causations, especially this last, according to whether the thing defined is cause or effect: assassin or victim, father or son.

"_ —— is a person who kills himself." "A parent is —— —— ——."

Route 21. *It behaves in this way.*

BEHAVIOR

"An extrovert is a person who —— —— ——."

"A puritan is someone who is, pretends to be, or is supposed to be —— in religion or morals."

"A dandy is a person who takes great pains to —— ——."

Route 22. *It is of this sex.*

S E X
  "A boar is — —— swine."
  "A hen is the —— of the common domestic fowl."

Route 23. *It serves this purpose.*

U s e
  "A hammer is — —— — beating, breaking, driving nails, etc."

Route 24. *He has this family connection with that person.*

F a m i l y   R e l a t i o n s
  "The brother of a person is the son of — — —— as that person."
  "A household is a —— establishment."

Route 25. *He has this legal connection with that person.*

L e g a l   R e l a t i o n s
  "A plaintiff is a person who brings suit into ——."
  "The owner is the person who has —— right to possession."
  "The person who is sued is called a ——."

These twenty-five routes are not the key to the riddle of the universe. They are a prescription for the more efficient use of words; and if the reader has the slightest qualm about any relationships he feels have been ignored, he should add them to this list, even though later they may be discarded as unnecessary. In fact, it would not be a bad idea to make the formal addition of Route 26, PRAGMATISM: *Any other kind of connection or connections, simple or complex, that you can think of.*

Often in conversation one uses a symbol which to the hearer is merely a sign, and definition is the process of changing such a sign into a symbol for the hearer, by giving him more information about its context. A practical advantage of attention to formal or informal definition is that it helps to create good manners in conversation, just as courtesy in directing a stranger is a sign of good manners in the street.

There was a school of theosophy that used to encourage its followers in the regular performance of a curious spiritual exercise. A fellow had to take a matchbox and slide out its inside drawer. He had to put this drawer on a table and sit down in front of it. He could not touch it, nor move. For an hour and a half he had to sit and contemplate this bit of a matchbox, with an empty eye and a vacant mind, after which time he turned his thoughts into more constructive channels. If he had been encouraged to consider the object's properties, and its relation to the rest of the world, with the help of the twenty-five routes that have just been described, he would have finished up with a far better appreciation of the nature of the matchbox, and would have had a far more interesting time over the thing.

Definition is not hard to explain or to practice, if one

remembers that we can get a bird's-eye view of all the possible ways of defining, and that every situation prescribes its own laws for choosing the route and the starting point.

Rules of thumb which will enable anyone to become a successful teacher or a more popular conversationalist can be laid down in one easy paragraph! When trying to explain anything, be patient until you find the common ground which is to be the starting point. Then get clearly before your own mind, and describe clearly to yourself, the three factors you must employ: what the common starting point is, what the destination is, and what kind of road you are going to follow from the one to the other. If at first you do not succeed, try a different road. Just as it is better, when talking to a deaf friend over the telephone, not to repeat "We're starting tomorrow," but to say the second time "We're beginning on Thursday," so it is better to make a habit of explaining things in a number of different ways. Repetition of the same ideas in the same words in the same place is deadening, in most circumstances. Most of us are too much tied to two or three of the definition routes, and this plight is one form of the error of being slaves to our words instead of controlling them.

So, if one wanted to end on a light note of uplift, one would say that the result of a variation of definition techniques will be the improvement or acquirement of two qualities which are social as well as intellectual assets. By taking another's standpoint one becomes more tolerant of his opinions and, therefore, a more pleasant person with whom to converse; and by insisting on getting as near as possible to the facts as well as they can be known, one becomes a straight thinker and a useful person to know.

Chief Points

When you are talking to someone about the best way for him to get from one part of town to another, it is necessary first of all to get agreement on two points:

(1) what place he is starting from
(2) which place he is going to

Then it is possible to give him a clear account of the road to take.

"Definition" is nothing more or less than the use of a certain road to take your hearer from a common referent to one which is new to him. The number of such roads is limited—in other words, our minds are able to make connections between one thought and another in only a limited number of ways. These ways may be listed; and the knowledge and conscious use of them will be seen to be of great value for the exchange of ideas.

Practice Exercises

I. In each of these exercises, put against the (2) phrase the number of the (1) phrase which in your opinion it most closely resembles, the criterion being the kind of way one noun is connected with another. Don't be afraid to give more than one answer.

A (1)

1. the corner of the room
2. the members of the family
3. the bag of coke
4. the consciousness of her presence
5. the air of the room
6. the Day of Judgment
7. the limousine of Mr. Montmorency
8. the cries of the morning
9. the wall of stone
10. the destruction of the hall
11. the importance of learning
12. the quality of mercy
13. the decision of the judge
14. the rules of a good life

A (2)

1. the salesmen of the company——
2. the thought of you——
3. the dress of silk——
4. the end of the street——
5. the field of corn——
6. the snows of yesteryear——
7. the time of parting——
8. the defense of the Tower——
9. the property of acidity——

B (1)

1. stone wall
2. cannon ball
3. parish church
4. lady friend
5. Boston lady
6. summer dress
7. square dance
8. committee business

B (2)

1. gold coin——
2. man servant——
3. London papers——
4. government work——
5. business purposes——
6. zigzag course——

II. Take stock of your own definition vocabulary; make a list of common English words which would be specially useful in connection with each one of the twenty-five definition routes described in Chapter Six. For example, a list for the fourth route might be: a, some, part, division, of. Ignore grammatical categories and do not try to make any list complete. Simply put down for every route a number (two to ten) of words which seem to you to have a clear connection with it.

7

METAPHOR: *BORROWING THE NAME OF ANOTHER THING*

JUST before the first World War a German scholar published a book called *The Philosophy of As If.* The German in the street, if he heard of the book at all, was probably just tickled by the title. But it angered many philosophers, for its main argument took the line that most of the things we talk and think about do not really exist and in our hearts we know they have no existence; they are used as metaphors.

We Speak and Think in Metaphors

This idea, that we do most of our talking in metaphors, should not make us angry. Rather, if it is true, should we pat ourselves on the back for beginning to realize the metaphorical nature of our language, and to realize how often, when we use the word "same," we have the im-

plications of "similar" at the back of our minds. For
speaking in metaphors is as old as words themselves,
and *acting* in metaphors as old as life. Lloyd Morgan's
chicken certainly acted this way, and possibly kept away
from all sorts of black-and-yellow things which were not
caterpillars at all. It may have deprived itself of some
delicious courses. Metaphor plays a part in our simplest
acts of perception: the effects upon our nerves of new
sights and sounds and smells are quickly compared with
our memories of similar effects in the past.

In this twentieth century we must try to avoid being
as stupid as that chicken. One good test of our success
lies in whether or not we can recognize when language
is being used metaphorically. And one of the marks of
wisdom is the faculty of recognizing what a big part
metaphors play in our life. For the time being the reader
may use his own conception of what a metaphor is.
(Think of a couple of examples.) Later in this chapter
I shall discuss the sorts of examples which are metaphorical in the conventional sense; but it is far more
important for us to see the workings of the metaphorical
process.

Not only is Metaphor the guiding principle in everybody's use of words; it is the essential principle of self-
preservation. "A burnt child dreads the fire." . . . "Once
bitten, twice shy." From earliest times, men of every race
have recognized the importance of this ability to carry
over memories of one thing to the contemplation of another thing we consider "similar." If a first lion scares

us, we do our best to keep away from a second. I was about to write that "we cannot help" this process—but as conscious human beings we *must* help it, by reflecting upon it.

On the domestic front, whenever we see a cat we only recognize what it is because we have seen other cats. Or, to take the events in their actual order, we carry over the name "cat" from past contexts and use it as a label for a part of a contemporary context. So, whenever we have dealings with a solid, breathing, furniture-brushing cat, and refer to him by the name "cat," we use that name to cover two ideas:

(1) the ways in which he is different from all other cats
(2) the ways in which he resembles all other cats

Every cat, every animal, every object, every experience is thus at the same time both unique and familiar.

Whenever one refers to an individual as a "man," one runs the risk of merely remembering that he is a male member of the human species and forgetting the wart on his nose, the talent for the saxophone, the overdraft at the bank, and all the et ceteras which piled up together render him unique. Every word in use represents a marriage between the general and the particular.

This sort of thing may lead to odd linguistic situations. In the olden days, people used to be named according to their occupations: John Baker, James Mason, William Smith. They changed their names, but the family name would stick; so in Middle English records we see references to "Walter Usher, tanner" and "Roger Carpenter, pepperer." A "white blackbird," too, is a curiosity—of orthology and ornithology alike: the words are as odd as the bird! How does it get its name? If the reader can give a neat verbal explanation of this linguistic oddity he is well on the road toward a mastery of the complexities of Metaphor.

When man started to talk he did not cut through his links with the past. It is easy to imagine, weaving about beneath the chicken's streamlined skull, obscure processes which are saying to the caterpillar: "Not this time, Mac. I tried you the other day, you know, and you didn't agree with me."

And, to remain in this howdah of playfulness a moment longer, just as the poet Omar, fondly gazing upon one of his girls, addressed her as "O moon of my delight that knowst no wane," so we can picture the chicken disgustedly contemplating, not a caterpillar, but perhaps a wingless hornet, and mutely saying: "O caterpillar . . . .!"

The difference in mental outlook between the two poets lies in the fact that Omar Khayyám was conscious of his beauty's difference from the moon as well as of her similarity; while with the chicken there is only similarity —and not even similarity: it is identity.

One could construct here a quite workable definition of "intelligence": the ability to see the unique qualities of an object as well as those it shares with other objects; the capacity to compare two things without confusing them; a faculty for using metaphorical language while remaining conscious that it *is* metaphorical; or, to squeeze in two terms before they are due, the ability to recognize the Tenor as well as the Vehicle of every metaphor we employ.

I hope that by now I have attached this chapter firmly to the fourth and shown that Metaphor is fundamental to the symbol-situation. But, even taking the word in its more restricted sense, as exemplified by bottlenecks and snakes in the grass, we use every one of our words metaphorically as well as literally. Our most basic words— like "leg," "foot," "give," "in," "take"—are used metaphorically more often than not; and it is easy to see why. When two things are similar, we may have the same name or two different names for them. Whether two similar things are called by one, or two, names is a linguistic accident, and different languages have such accidents in different places.

Take for example the English word "head," the central referent of which is symbolized in French by *tête*. My head, *ma tête*. The head of the cabbage, *la tête du chou*. All right so far, but: a head of celery, *un pied* (foot) *de céleri;* the head of a cane, *la pomme* (apple, *pommel*) *d'une canne;* the head of an ax, *le fer* (iron) *d'une hache* —and so on. This is to illustrate the point that different languages have such accidents in different places.

In the discussion of different aspects of language— signs, symbols, contexts, definitions—it is convenient to attach each aspect to some archetype or representative example. I hope that the caterpillar, Schenectady, Australia, and the City Hall have already served a useful purpose; although, of course, there is always the danger that they will be used to oversimplify instead of as mnemonic pointers to the complexities to which they refer. It is difficult, however, to keep our perspective without some such anchors for our thoughts; without some classic examples of animal learning to remind us of those fundamentals of any sign-situation which are at the roots of all our use of language; without the Triangle of Reference to typify for us the way language works when it is used scientifically; or without those routes from Grand Central Station to recall to us the ways in which our symbols are connected in their contexts.

Similarly, an example of a metaphor is needed. This is a typical metaphor in the accepted sense: "That man is a wolf." Or, to take a more complex metaphor, "He is a wolf in sheep's clothing." These metaphors will be examined later, but first we must devote a page or two to shifts of meaning that are not metaphorical, in preparation for an attack from another angle upon Metaphor proper.

Obvious Shifts of Meaning

In calling a man a wolf, one is clearly taking advantage of the fact that men and wolves have already been named and classified, and making a cross-classification. This is the difference between the "metaphor" and an ordinary symbol—the metaphor is really a double metaphor: "that man who resembles men I have seen before and who also resembles wolves." Before anatomizing the metaphor of convention, which is really a far simpler question than the metaphorical matters we have gone into previously, I must step aside for a moment and consider certain sense-changes which are not metaphorical. These examples will not only throw light upon the functionings of metaphor; they will also reinforce the earlier discussion of shifts of meaning with some picturesque and comparatively concrete illustrations.

A missionary who was preparing a dictionary of the African dialect of his sphere of operations wrote: "I remember on one occasion wanting the word for Table. There were five or six boys standing round, and, tapping the table with my forefinger, I asked, 'What is this?' One boy said it was a *dodele;* another that it was an *etanda;* a third stated that it was *bokali;* a fourth that it was *elamba;* and the fifth said it was *meza.* These various words we wrote in our notebooks, and congratulated ourselves that we were working among a people who possessed so rich a language that they had five words for one article.

"One lad had thought we wanted the word for tapping; another understood we were seeking the word for the material of which the table was made; another had the idea that we required the word for hardness; another thought we wished for a name for that which covered the table; and the last, not being able, perhaps, to think of anything else, gave us the word *meza*, table—the very word we were seeking."

Here was a physical context in which five factors stood out with especial prominence: A, tap; B, wood; C, hard; D, cover; E, table. The missionary himself was thinking particularly of E, and so when he heard the symbols for A, B, C, and D he confused all four of them with E. This story illustrates the ease with which a symbol may be shuffled from one part of a context to another part of the same context. (In Metaphor, as we shall see, the symbol jumps from one context to a completely different one, on the strength of a similarity between certain factors in the two contexts.)

Years ago, New England recipe books used to tell their housewives to "take three blurps of molasses." A "blurp" was the noise made as the molasses came out of the jug.

The "knot" which now means "one nautical mile per hour" originally meant a knot on a line. Sailors measured the speed of their vessel by paying out this line, which had a knot for every fifty feet. The line was paid out for half a minute and then the knots were counted. The calculation of distance covered in an hour came later.

Sometimes we give the same name to factors in a context which are not only different, but in a kind of opposition to each other. The French word *hôte*, for example, signifies either guest or host. Our verb "rent" may stand either for the taking or the letting go aspect of the renting operation.

In the fourth chapter were considered certain types of shift which occur within psychological contexts, and here we are looking at symbols whose referents may be said to belong to physical contexts. We use in everyday life many symbols that have jumped from one part of a physical context to another: "redcap" from the garment to the functionary; "beads" from the prayers to the objects handled in accompaniment to the prayers; "whistle" from the instrument to the sound; "entrance" from the action to the place, and so on. These are such crude jumps that they cause few communicative troubles, and they are only of semantic interest when we reflect upon the tricks of thought they exemplify, and use them as pointers which may help us to spot more difficult ambiguities.

By far the most troublesome of these shifts from one factor in a context to another are those that occur in our symbolizations of mental or perceptive processes. Such words jump from a psychological to a physical context, and vice versa. ("My girl's a vision, and yours is a sight," says the old chestnut.) These symbols, such as "seeing," "hearing," "learning," "knowledge," confuse us very seriously if we do not take care to discover which particular factor (or stage) in the process they are referring to at the moment. But apart from this special difficulty, symbol-shifts among the various factors in a physical context are not much of a problem; and they provide a good introduction to the simplest form of a conventional metaphor, which involves two physical contexts.

The Mechanics of Metaphor

"That wolf"—"that wolf in sheep's clothing": the peculiarity of a metaphor proper is that it takes a symbol which represents a referent in a certain (e. g. animal) context, and uses it to represent a referent in a completely different (human) sort of context. Wolves belong to the wilds, and wool belongs to sheep, but we have no difficulty in understanding when their symbols are borrowed for use in a totally human context. We have already seen why. Any *word,* if we look upon it as something listed in a dictionary, has scores of possibilities. When it is at work, a context pins it down and makes it more specific. (Multiple definition, the habit of surveying representative examples of these possible uses, helps tremendously to prepare us to select those uses which are relevant in a given context. The last chapter of this book will discuss the necessity of practicing multiple definition on whole sentences and paragraphs.)

No word in use represents all the senses it is capable of representing. It is as if words were tents which are never used except as umbrellas, or so many Man-mountain Deans which spend their lives wrestling kittens with their little finger. The Swedish philologist, Gustav Stern, whose *Meaning and Change of Meaning* is recommended to those interested in the application of semantics to the philology of English, has explained this very clearly: "If a builder is speaking of *bricks* as a possible material for facing a building, he is probably thinking most of their color and external aspect; if he is speaking of bricks as an alternative material for foundations, he is thinking of their durability and resistance to high pressure; if he is discussing the number of bricks likely to be required for a certain construction, he is turning his attention mostly to their size; and if he is asking about the number of bricks delivered last week, he will be thinking about them as entities, without paying any attention, for the moment, to their characteristics. In this way different elements within the range of a word will on different occasions occupy a central position, because the characteristics of the referent which are apprehended through them are relevant to the momentary context."

Let us put it this way. An object has characteristics A, B, C, D, E, etc. When we use its name in speech we generally concentrate on one or two of these characteristics. If a certain man has characteristic W, say, and wolves also have characteristic W, it is quite natural, when we are thinking especially of this characteristic, to call the man a wolf. The same man may also possess characteristic M, a mild appearance; that is how it happens that a man is called a wolf in sheep's clothing. This metaphor must have been dynamite when it was first used. It was forceful enough to be taken up in a big way, till now it is merely a bromide, a cliché. Awolfinsheepsclothing—it is practically one word, so that many people who use it do not think of the animals at all. For them the metaphor is unintentional—dead.

A child is not acquainted with a very large number of things, and with a narrow range of objects to choose from he is not always able to find an apt comparison; so his metaphors are often wild and poetical. The adult's use of metaphor is safer and less surprising, because he has stopped thinking.

Characteristic C of the caterpillar left traces in the chicken's nervous system, so that it regarded other possessors of the same characteristic with a bias. We, too, on meeting a new acquaintance, are often influenced by our memory of an old one. Sometimes we give it the same name. That vertebra which supports our skull we call *Atlas,* in memory of the legendary giant who held the weight of the world upon his shoulders. A hoisting apparatus with a long neck and a hanging rope is a *crane,* because it reminds us of a certain bird—the foreign words *Kran* (German and Swedish) and *grue* (French) provide evidence that other nationalities have seen the same resemblance. Metaphorical names which are particularly appropriate tend to be adopted for general use. Then, in the normal sense of that word, they cease to be metaphors, and their new sense takes its place within the accepted range of the original word.

When thrifty Benjamin Franklin was seven years old, a day came when he had a holiday and a pocketful of pennies. He went to the store and bought a whistle, giving the shopkeeper all the money he had. The whistle delighted him for awhile, but his brothers and sisters and cousins all teased him about it, explaining that he could have got it at a quarter the price. Franklin described the incident in a letter: "I cried with vexation; and the reflection gave me more chagrin than the whistle gave me pleasure. This, however, was afterwards of use to me, the impression continuing on my mind; so that often, when I was tempted to buy some unnecessary thing, I said to myself, Don't give too much for the whistle; and I saved my money."

All the objects or achievements which Benjamin later compared to his whistle had in common this characteristic: they were too dear at the price he was being asked to pay for them. Metaphors can be emotive—we compare things with our feelings as well as with our brains. Objects which we call *good* or *lovely* or *beautiful* are likely to be used in emotive metaphors.

"All beauty lies in the beholder's eye."

Tone as well as Feeling can play its part in emotive metaphors. Mr. Blotton took refuge in Metaphor as the most graceful way of saving his face. He was not unlike that clergyman, of uncompromising beliefs but kindly and timid soul, who told his congregation that "if they didn't repent, as it were, they would be damned, so to speak."

At the beginning of this chapter, it was suggested that every time we use the name of even the commonest object—a chair, a table, or a man—this name represents the fusion in our heads of two different thoughts, which Peirce differentiated by the two handy names of *type* and *token*. When you pay back the dollar you owe some-one, do you return *the same* dollar or not? The answer, of course, is that in general terms it is, in particular terms it is not, the same. It is the same type, but not the same token. Similarly with chairs, or tables, or men. Their name stands for the particular object which stands be-fore us, and also for the general idea of all the similar thoughts we have had.

A metaphorical symbol represents a fusion, too, but in this case the referents which here are fused are taken from different spheres of experience.

Some of our literary professors have misled us about Metaphor. It is not an extra beauty stuck on to language —it *is* language. So much ink has been spilt over meta-phors; so much uninspired poetry has been written in prose about the beauties of metaphorical language; so much time has been wasted making a distinction between similes and metaphors which is hardly worth making— yet we lack in our ordinary vocabulary the words neces-sary to describe how a metaphor functions. In *The Phi-losophy of Rhetoric,* I. A. Richards names the two differ-ent factors in a metaphor the Tenor and the Vehicle. It is quite difficult to see the distinction at first and to get accustomed to using these two symbols properly; the mastery of them implies mastery of the fundamentals of Metaphor.

Tenor and Vehicle

Let us borrow preliminary definitions of these terms from the *Concise Oxford Dictionary*. Tenor is "the general purport, drift (of speech, writing, etc."). Vehicle is "a thing used as a medium for thought or feeling or action."

What would be the Tenor and the Vehicle in the whistle and the wolf-in-sheep's-clothing metaphors?

Tenor: "This hat (house, auto, concert ticket, fishing rod) for which I am being asked to pay too much."

Vehicle: "That whistle for which I paid too much."

Tenor: "This man, who behaves in such a gentle way, but is cruel and violent at heart."

Vehicle: "That wild animal of the dog family, which has a ferocious nature, lives on sheep and other animals, but just now is disguising its own harsh fur by wearing over it the soft woolly coat of a sheep, a gentle and timid animal."

This distinction between Tenor and Vehicle helps a great deal in one's control of language, if a little trouble is taken to master it. It would be a horrible crime of punning to suggest another metaphor—"Caruso was a caravan of song"—as a device for remembering which factor is which!

All of us constantly speak in metaphors. Whenever we do so, we concentrate upon a few of the vehicle's characteristics; but its other qualities hang around on the fringes of our minds, and so we often get more kick from a metaphorical word than from a literal one. It is very easy now to describe the way we use metaphors in practice. A post, for example, generally has these characteristics: it is A, round; B, straight; C, fixed; D, upright; E, solid; F, wooden. Anybody or anything which has one or more of these characteristics can be called a post. (Someone can catch me up on this example, but I wanted to put the thing as simply as possible.) The reader can test the truth of this description by thinking of a friend and calling him or her each one of these names; an acid, a cheese, a ledger, a swan, a wheel. Then think up reasons to justify these metaphors; or even two sets of reasons, complimentary and uncomplimentary. Probably a Christmas parlor game could be thought up along these lines.

If we cannot make friends and become high executives, and if we blame our failure upon our poor mastery of words, our plight is not due to the smallness of our vocabulary. Miracles can be worked with a couple of thousand words, and the most tongue-tied person is constantly using five or ten times that number. Perhaps we pause and search for recondite synonyms when an apt and simple metaphor could drive the nail firmly home. We are weak, not because our vocabulary is inadequate, but because we are stale in the way we use it.

Chief Points

A metaphor is the comparison, in one word, of two things from different fields of experience. In the statement "that girl is a cat," the word "cat" is a metaphor. In this, as in every metaphor, there are two parts: the Tenor and the Vehicle. The Tenor in this example is a cruel, ill-humored young woman; the Vehicle, a cruel, ill-humored animal (though this is a false thing to say about cats). It is very important to see the connection between the way in which we make use of a metaphor and the way we make use of any general name.

Practice Exercises

Write a brief description of the Tenor and the Vehicle of each metaphor italicized below; and state in each case a number of characteristics which Tenor and Vehicle share in common.

1. Borrowing *dulls the edge* of husbandry.—Shakespeare.
2. Ah, what a *dusty* answer gets the soul when *hot* for certainties in this our life!—Meredith.
3. Under the opening *eyelids* of the morn.—Milton.
4. A wit's a *feather*, and a chief a *rod*;
   An honest man's the noblest work of God.—Pope.
5. E'en in our ashes live their wonted *fires*.—Gray.
6. Chewing the *food* of sweet and bitter fancy.—Shakespeare.
7. Give, oh give me back my *heart*!—Byron.
8. The *paths* of glory lead but to the grave.—Gray.
9. The *primrose way* to the everlasting bonfire.—Shakespeare.

10. Ladies, whose bright eyes
    Rain influence.—Milton.

11. A few more years shall *roll*.—Bonar.

12. Or to take arms against a *sea* of troubles,
    And by opposing end them?—Shakespeare.

13. It may be said that his wit *shines* at the expense
    of his memory.—Le Sage.

14. No creature *smarts* so little as a fool.—Pope.

15. Fame is the *spur* that the clear spirit doth raise
    To scorn delights, and live laborious days.—Milton.

16. Bread is the *staff* of life.—Swift.

17. Man is his own *star*.—John Fletcher.

18. Facts are *stubborn* things.—Smollett.

19. Come, give us a *taste* of your quality; come, a passionate speech.—Shakespeare.

8

FICTIONS: *THE STUFF THAT DREAMS ARE MADE ON*

*My proposals were all accepted by the sub-commit-
tee. Only I was obliged to insert two phrases about
"duty" and "right" into the Preamble to the Statutes, ditto "truth," "morality," and "justice," but
these are placed in such a way that they can do no
harm.*

KARL MARX, *in a letter to Friedrich Engels,
September 7, 1864.*

THE man on the street corner who says there "ain't
no justice" speaks more truly than he knows. There
has never been any such thing. Justice is a Fiction, along
with its fellows—Friendship, Discipline, Democracy, Liberty, Socialism, Isolationism, and Appeasement. You cannot point to their referents. It is hard even to describe
what is meant by them, unless one takes the course of
substituting one Fiction for another. Should all such
words be "sent to the doghouse"?

This, the last *theoretical* chapter of my book, must
also be the most tentative. I have played with half a
dozen different ways of presenting its facts and ideas,
and must emphasize now that this chapter's purpose
will be fulfilled if the reader follows my thought and sees
what I am driving at. You may accompany me as friend
or foe: all I hope to do is to display some parts of the

problem. A discussion of semantics should end on a humble note, as it began. I think my advice on how to deal with Fictions is sound and practical so far as it goes.

Headaches for Semanticians

My plan here is to illustrate the general nature of the problem by examples, to discuss briefly some questions of generalization and scientific and semiscientific classification—so as to be able to dismiss those problems from the present discussion—and then to discuss Bentham's and other methods of pinning our abstract language down to reality. Luckily, we have already gone into the business of multiple definition, which is obviously an invaluable technique for helping us to decide what our abstract words are talking about.

Speaking of multiple definition, two different definitions of *Fiction* should be examined here.

Fiction. 1. Works of literature, such as stories and novels, which consist of invented narratives.

2. A word which refers to an invention of the mind, and is not the name of any object or any specific sense-experience.

Fiction will be used here in its second sense. (I shall capitalize it for the sake of clarity.) One cannot escape the problem by saying that all Fictions are emotive, and so must only be used for poetical purposes. A word like *control* has evident referential value, and so has *heat.*

Both are the names of Fictions. Writing of *heat,* Professor H. Levy says, "Scientific textbooks will tell you that 'Heat is a mode of Motion,' or 'Heat arises from the agitation of the molecules of the substance,' or 'Heat is a form of energy,' all of which goes to show that in point of fact there is no such independent 'thing' as 'heat.' "

This word is used just to express the fact that a given substance is going through a certain process. Certainly the process or thing or whatever-we-like-to-call-it named "heat" has no independent existence apart from substances. "The idea that it has such an existence," says Professor Levy, "is a fiction encouraged by the separate term Heat."

Control is in the same boat. A country aunt who was being driven from New York to Boston nervously asked her nephew if he was never afraid that he would lose control of his car. He said, "Yes," very seriously. "In fact, I'm already three installments behind on my payments." Here the two kinds of *control* seem to have little but their name in common. In both cases the word seems to be acting like a metaphor which has a tenor but no vehicle. What are we to do with such words? Some enthusiasts suggest throwing them away and never using them again. I would like to see them try—they might as well try to split atoms with bows and arrows.

Pioneer chemists long ago used to talk about *phlogiston,* which they said was the "inflammable principle" which existed in combination in all combustible bodies.

If something contained phlogiston, it would burn; if not, not. Phlogiston was a Fiction, though many of the ideas which were attached to "it" are true of oxygen. The word *electricity* comes from a Greek word meaning *amber*. (If you rub a piece of amber with a woolen cloth, it will have the power to pick up light things.) Does such a thing as electricity exist?

Even the *waves* on the sea may be said to be Fictions. A wave is not a single moving mass of water, but an appearance created by little particles of water that jog up and down in a circular movement. That is why, if you drop a piece of colored cellophane onto a wave, it does not dash out of sight in a few minutes.

In biology, scores of fictitious hormones have been hatched during the present century. Dr. Oscar Riddle has exposed a number of these "ghosts," as he calls them, and believes the number of definitely established front-lobe hormones to be small—five at the most.

Politicians are more conservative in their vocabulary than scientists. Although, judging by the quotation at the head of this chapter, Marx himself seems to have seen Duty, Right, Truth, Morality, and Justice as nothing but five Fictions, he was forced by his collaborators to pay some respect to them in the framing of the Statutes of the first Workingmen's International Association. Many politicians dote on Fictions of every kind. Read any one of the speeches made by Ramsay Mac-Donald in his last five years and you will see flocks of Fictions plunging around like mules in a mine.

Generalizations

There is one kind of symbol which we must definitely put to one side, or it will smother any attempt to get our teeth into the real Fictions. This is the sort of word which stands for a class of things—every "common noun," as we call them grammatically. Every time we use a symbol like *coin, money, cat, animal, creature,* in its general (its type as opposed to its token) sense, we are using an abstraction. The psychologist Koffka found a number of students who, when the word *coin* was mentioned, conjured up "an image of a coin, but of no special denomination." We must draw a line between such Generalizations and words like *truth, justice,* and *control,* which are, or stand for, Fictions.

Let us suppose that there is a fly in your house, one unique particular fly, which we will refer to as *the fly.* Near your right hand there is also some special object we will call *This.* These are very specific things. The name for the most "general" thing one can possibly think of is the word *thing.* Now here are five specific referents: General Chiang Kai-shek, the fly, Premier Benito Mussolini, Secretary Joseph Stalin, This. One could easily take each of their five names and cover it with a more general name, then a more general one still, until one reaches the supergeneral *thing.* Generality obviously goes in stages, like steps up a ladder.

We pick up our knowledge of generalizations in two ways. In our own private experience we encounter creatures like wasps, flies, and cockroaches and learn to talk about them; but there is also the public experience which is embodied in the sciences. Entomology has all our domestic insects classified and put in their places among thousands of other insects. So our own groping generalizations are continually yielding to the generalizations of the scientists. We learn to fit our own world in with theirs.

We need not consider generalization any further. Man's tidy mind is constantly trying to arrange his Fictions according to similar hierarchies; but they refuse to fall in, except for limited purposes when marshaled by specialists. My dictionary tells me that *hate* is an emotion; that *emotion* is feeling or affection; and that *affection* is an emotion. Granted that emotive words and psychological terms are especially difficult; yet other kinds of Fictions show peculiar slipperinesses of their own. They may emulate the sliding scale of "see" and "interpret," and operate at different times on different levels. A *control* may be a lever, or a lever which controls other levers, or the man who controls the controls, or his controller, and so on. It is clear that we need a very flexible technique if we are to deal effectively with such goings on; and here semantics owes much to that great pioneer in linguistic psychology, Jeremy Bentham.

The Bogeys of Bentham

Bentham, who died in 1832, never throughout his long life ceased to resent his memories of his own childhood, in which phantoms and Fictions and bogeys of all kinds had loomed dreadfully. The malicious servants of little Jeremy's family had planted hobgoblins for him everywhere, even in the household's two "shrines of necessary pilgrimage," which they said were invisibly occupied by "Tom Dark" and "Rawhead and Bloody Bones." "I kept away for weeks from the spots I have mentioned; and when suffering was intolerable, I fled to the fields. . . . Even now," said Bentham sixty or seventy years later, "though my judgment is wholly free, my imagination is not wholly so."

Bentham's revolt against the tyranny of Fictions took the form of a prolonged study of them. He examined their names, pried into the work they did, and invented ways of rendering them manageable. Among his thousands upon thousands of manuscript papers he left detailed instructions for dealing with Fictions: methods which would either blow such words to pieces, by proving them to be nothing but bluff, or else anchor them down to solid earth.

Bentham's *Theory of Fictions* describes his formulas fully. Briefly, this is his line of attack: when you get a statement or pseudo statement which is hard to understand because it is puffed full of abstractions, do two things with it. First, paraphrase it, using the simplest and most concrete words possible. You are not distorting the original when you do this; you are getting as much of the meaning of the original as it is in your power to get, and expressing it in terms which are "nearer to reality." The second operation, which we have mentioned before, is what Bentham called "archetypation." This consists in picking out the most abstract words of the original, the biggest sinners among the Fictions, and providing them with archetypes. Something was said in the fourth chapter about this method, but now it may be explained more concisely: treat these words as if they were metaphors, and provide each one of them with a vehicle. *Control*, for instance, might be considered as representing a pair of reins in use, or a steering wheel. If one does not like these images, and says they do not at all represent what *control* means, then one must think of a picture which does. If this cannot be done, one's general idea of the word in question is probably far woollier than it need be.

It is best to draw pictures of these archetypes. The method of archetypation is of most value to people keenly interested in *words* as well as in what they say—people who know how to make the distinction between what a word pretends to be doing and what it actually does—and to educators, and to anybody else who realizes its limitations. For obviously an archetype cannot tell the full story. It would be sad indeed if we thought of Truth as merely an arrow sticking in a bull's-eye, or of Equality as nothing but an even pair of scales. An archetype (sometimes more than one) is a necessary factor in the comprehension of any word, but it represents only the root sense, from which the word will grow and branch into multitudinous diversities. A wise knowledge of the word will demand an awareness of the ramifications and depths and subtleties it has developed through the minds of philosophers and poets and great men.

However, a rather crude idea of the senses of Fictions is better than a vague one. We need a picture dictionary which will illustrate, not our concrete words, but our abstractions. One is quite right to insist on the peculiar and unique sense of a Fiction every time it is used, but we must try to stop its root sense from floating around over too wide a surface. When Fictions are used, we need to be able to see where they stand in relation to reality.

Defects in our language machine should be regarded as direct threats to our sanity. Semantics would be worth investigation if it did nothing but make us conscious of these defects. This subject can be turned to very queer ends by people who already had a gleam in their eye before they met it. But if its principles were taken into schools, by teachers with their feet on the ground, it could do great things toward solving our language problems.

Few people deny that we have such problems, and least of all educators. Teachers of English in schools and colleges do many wonderful things for their students, instructing them in the rules of rhetoric, encouraging them to write short stories and radio continuity; but many thoughtful teachers confess to a feeling that their courses lack a something which is not easy to define—some sort of a touchstone of what is what.

This lack takes a more serious form in our institutions for the mentally unfit. Many doctors are groping after some kind of verbal retraining which will help to restore to their patients—some, of course, not all—their mental grip on reality. The answers to such questions must be based on principles such as those I have tried to formulate in this book. To realize the nature of the problem is to take a great stride toward its solution. The most practical first step is for the individual to do all he can to master the theory of how language functions.

But what do I mean by pinning our words down to reality? Surely *reality* itself is an enormous Fiction! Yes, but, like any other Fiction, it can be given an archetype. When you dream of a house you are dreaming of your own body. Let us follow this metaphor. Reality is the traffic that goes on through the doors and windows between the inside and the outside of the house. The most real things are those which are nearest our sills and walls and thresholds—such perceptions and simple sign- and symbol-situations as were discussed in earlier chapters. The solid comfortable objects that we see around us, and the simple, ever-present sensations we feel within—these are the reality to which everything else must be linked. Words are the links.

Some of our Fictions are only a step from reality, just one level away. Others are farther and farther distant. Each sphere of thought has a special road (forgive the mixture of metaphors) of its own, with its special terminology ranked row by row in different levels of fictionality. But, as we have seen, a word can often change its level. In the linguistic sphere, for example, as Bertrand Russell has aptly put it: when we see the *sun* and say its name we speak in the primary language (to stick to Russell's vocabulary); when we utter the word *word*, however, we speak in the secondary language; talk about the *secondary language* is in the tertiary language; discussing the *tertiary language* makes us use the quaternary language—and so on.

Just as one finds it hard, when discussing metaphors, to discover a word which is not a metaphor, so, in the examination of Fictions, it is hard to find a word that is not a Fiction. However, in practice—when one is talking not about language but about something else—it is generally a simple matter to decide that some words are farther from reality than others. I will discuss an artificial example: "I laugh, and go to the red chair."

Let us agree for purposes of this illustration that every symbol—each separate word—has a referent. For the benefit of those who prefer to consider referents as tangible things, let us add that "every symbol has a referent, real or metaphorical." Now, as soon as one looks at any referent by itself, one sort of solidifies it—turns it into a thing; somewhat as a word belonging to any grammatical part of speech can become a noun, as *the* and *of* become nouns when one says: "*The* and *of* are the words I am talking about."

I will take four words and look at them separately: *laugh, to, red, chair*—a verb, a preposition, an adjective, and a noun. Beside every symbol which is not a noun I will put its noun form, because, as we have seen, every symbol considered in isolation becomes a noun.

Laugh: "a laugh." Alice met in Wonderland a Cheshire cat which had the knack of leaving its grin behind after the cat had vanished. But *my* laugh has no existence apart from me, and a laugh considered as something in itself is an abstraction, a Fiction.

To: the noun form is "approach." The concrete objects in an approach are: one object that is moving and another that is relatively at rest. Therefore, if you consider *approach* as something independent, and do not take these objects into account, you are making an abstraction, a Fiction.

Red: "redness." You cannot have *redness* without having something which is *red*. Therefore, *red*, as a thing-in-itself, is a Fiction, whether it is considered as a part of the chair or a part of our eyes.

Chair: a chair is a chair. It has a solid existence and is not a Fiction.

This may seem very exasperating—a good demonstration of the absurdity of considering a symbol apart from its context, and of several other semantic crimes; but I think it can give the reader an idea of the point at which fictionality begins. The only way to clarify the meanings of difficult and abstract words is to show their connection with concrete situations; and the test of what is a concrete situation is the evidence of our senses.

So we need not, for this purpose, worry over whether

chairs are not Fictions too, if they are nothing but lumps of space with things like electrons whizzing about inside them. People do wrangle with one another over the question of whether Things are not really Events; so, should they be *called* Things? This is a world of action, motion, change, they say. Should not language recognize this fact, and set out to equip itself with a grammar and a vocabulary that would reflect the changes of the outside world? Should not all nouns really be verbs? And so on. This pother need not detain us. If Things are really Events, then they are that kind of event that happens slowly enough to be called a Thing.

The fictional nature of *laugh, to,* and *red* in such a down-to-earth sentence as my example is of only theoretical interest: they are so close to the nonfictional level that they could not cause much trouble in communication. As for abstract words in general, most of us need, not to use our Fictions any the less, but to change our attitude toward them. We must always be ready to translate our utterances into concrete terms which hold fewer possibilities of difference of opinion. Taking a fictional word by itself, we must be able to treat it as a metaphor, and get firmly attached to the idea of thinking up some object or objects as an archetype for the notion, some object that will serve as the Vehicle for the metaphor. With these two devices should be mentioned the practice of multiple definition, which helps one to realize the potential richness of the Fiction under examination. It is best to take the adjectival form of the Fiction for this purpose. For archetypation, take the noun, which acts "as if" it were the name of a solid object: "Freedom is like a ——"; only the archetype, the Vehicle of the metaphor, has to be supplied. But, in doing multiple definitions, the adjective is more practicable: "A man is free

when he ——
when he ——
when he ——"

and so on.

The ability to regard a Fiction as a metaphor strengthens our control over our symbols and the things for which they stand. The recognition of a metaphor is a mark of intelligence. We all know silly people who find it very hard, not only to realize that Fictions are metaphors, but even to remember that fiction in its usual sense is an invention—that the stories they read in novelettes or see on movie screens or hear over the radio did not actually happen. I knew an old trade-union man who thought that with a little education one of his colleagues would do well as a leader, so he started him off by giving him *Oliver Twist* to read. The young fellow got so excited that he forgot the immediate class struggle and wanted to go and picket the workhouse where Oliver was being mistreated. We are in far greater danger of being seduced by our Fictions. When we constantly talk about them in terms which encourage us to believe they really exist, it is not always easy to retain the necessary "as-if" attitude toward them.

A word (or phrase) stands for a Fiction, then, when it

is not to be taken as the name for, or the direct description of, a concrete experience. (Have you noticed the shift the word *Fiction* keeps making in this chapter, from referent to symbol and back again? Awareness of this shift is the important thing: it is not always necessary to add "the name of" or "stands for" every time such a relationship is implied. This would become tiresome, like putting "a photograph of Durham Castle" instead of just "Durham Castle" on a picture postcard.) *Control, justice,* and *love* are examples of Fictions.

Gyps, Guesses, and Ghosts

There is one more complication. We have to distinguish between three different kinds of Fictions, which I shall call respectively *gyps, guesses,* and *ghosts.*

Gyp has no implication of dishonesty here: it is a Briticism. Gyps in certain English universities are those tireless men who go around doing useful jobs like cleaning people's shoes. Gyps as Fictions are little mechanics like *a* and *the* and *if,* which might be looked upon as busy little gnomes bustling round and tying up words in the right places. They can best be described in terms of the work they do.

Our great problem with such symbols is to realize that they are a problem. Can we imagine a situation in which we had to explain the difference between *a* and *the?* Suppose we wanted to demonstrate their use to a foreigner whose language did not possess similar words. (There are languages which do not.) Our best bet would probably be to do something like pointing to a moon picture and a star picture; and to say to him *"the* moon" and *"a* star," relying upon his sense of arithmetic and knowledge of the celestial bodies to help us out. The simplest way of finding a referent for *if* is to think of a sentence containing the word, and to express the same thought without using *if,* thus defining that little symbol in terms of its function.

These ten English words are used far more frequently than any others: a, and, I, in, is, it, of, that, the, to. All of them except (for obvious reasons) *I* occur among the Herodotus list of twenty-two words in the fifth chapter. If we regard such symbols, "operators" as C. K. Ogden calls them, as Fictions, can we find archetypes for them? Yes, if we want to; we can translate the mental operations they symbolize into nouns, so that *the* might become *specificity, of* become *attachment* or *relationship, near* become *propinquity.* Such translation would result in very complex Fictions of the "ghost" kind, and it would be an amusing and brain-twisting occupation to furnish them with unambiguous archetypes.

However, it is more useful to become as a little child again, and to re-create the sorts of contexts from which we must have learned to use these words acceptably; and also to collect examples in which these little operators seem to be used in different ways. The exploration of the jobs these gyps perform gives an admirable approach to the subjects of mathematics and logic. Mathematics might be introduced through some such list as:

and, as, from, less, more, one, over, seven, two; and logic: a, but, if, is, or, the.

By *guesses,* my second type of Fictions, I mean the hypotheses of the scientist. As a basis for experiment, he guesses that a certain element or something exists. He gives it a name: "phlogiston" or "electricity" or "electron" or "hormone" or "chromosome." Then he says that, if it does exist, so-and-so will happen when he does such-and-such. He tries the test, and so-and-so does happen; or perhaps it does not. So the scientists' Fictions are constantly being either verified or scrapped. Sometimes a new discovery makes necessary a complete reorientation, and the fainthearted, rather than undertake to learn a new terminology, flee into monasteries.

Our main concern here, however, is with the *ghosts.* They are, comparatively speaking, firm and fast and unchanging. There is no shadow of doubt about whether their referents really exist: they just don't. They are Youth and Goodness and Beauty; Control and Government and Authority. We must find archetypes for them. From concrete life they came, and to concrete life they must be made to return.

Since, as we have seen, archetypation is only the starting point in the study of a Fiction, we should not in seeking archetypes pay too much attention to the etymology of such a word. Sometimes they have not traveled too far. The word "explain," for example, means from its literal Latin derivation *to spread out flat;* which is not bad. But, on the other hand, we get a word like "ambition" which literally means *going about* (people used to go about canvasing votes). This is not good enough. A better metaphorical archetype would be something like a balloon, or even a rocket, to which the subject was attached.

Abstract words often give birth to archetypes of their own. *Youth,* for example, has produced *a youth,* a young man. Certain levers in an airplane are called *controls,* and the abstract art of *advertisement* produces tangible *advertisements* on walls and in journals. So, in finding archetypes for our Fictions, we are simply continuing a process already begun. We are getting our feet on the ground, which is a good thing to do.

In addition to their sense values, our most important Fictions have aesthetic and ethical implications—they are emotive as well as referential. It is not easy to live up to such words as Beauty, Democracy, Equality, Goodness, Justice, Liberty, Reason, and Truth, which represent the best that is in our tradition and our hopes for the future. Just as our primitive words made us better than animals, these will make us better than ourselves, for they add up, it seems to me, to a referent which is nothing less than a world society of friendly and liberal states, militantly policed against the abuse of force; whose citizens, all assured by law of a certain minimum of material comfort and security, reconcile individualism with social consciousness, permit no discrimination against sex or class or race, and enrich their lives with things of beauty and with discoveries from the wisdom of the present and the past—citizens who, like us indeed, have a limitless task, with unlimited powers of learning to do it better. "Here is God's plenty."

Chief Points

The earlier parts of this book have made it clear how necessary it is to take into account the Context of a word. Looking at a Symbol by itself is frequently the cause of serious error.

However, in the English language there is an increasing tendency for every word to be pinned onto some separate bit of experience, and to get some sort of general sense which may be looked at independently.

Among the different sorts of Symbols, those which seem to have the strongest separate existence are our "nouns"—the names of things. Men and women and cats and pigs and houses are units in themselves. But a great number of our "names of things" are false names, because they have no things at the back of them. Truth, Goodness, Beauty, Attention, Control are examples of such words. They are the names of Fictions.

There are two rules which make us able to put Fictions to work without letting them get out of control.

(1) Be ready to put any statement which is full of Fictions into simpler language, using symbols representative of more solid things.

(2) Taking a Fiction separately, get into the way of looking upon it as a metaphor which has no Vehicle; and be ready to give it a Vehicle.

Practice Exercises

    I.   Write down twenty abstract nouns expressing what you take to be the root sense of the following prepositions: about, across, after, against, among, at, before, between, by, down, from, in, off, on, over, through, to, under, up, with.

   II.   Draw archetypes for the twenty abstract nouns of I.

  III.   Collect different uses of each of the following adjectives: beautiful, democratic, equal, free, good, just, reasonable, true.

  IV.   Translate the eight adjectives of III into nouns, and describe in words simple concrete situations which would illustrate the root senses of your eight nouns.

9

APPLIED SEMANTICS: *BASIC ENGLISH*

One of the unanticipated achievements of the twenty-first century was the rapid diffusion of Basic English as the lingua franca of the world.
H. G. WELLS, *The Shape of Things to Come.*

WHEN C. K. Ogden and I. A. Richards were studying the problems of definition, in the course of writing *The Meaning of Meaning*, they practiced defining all sorts of words and found themselves using a very limited set of definition-words. This suggested the possibility of inventing a complete language with a very small vocabulary, which would cover all the words outside its own range by describing, defining, or expanding them. Such a definition vocabulary, instead of admitting symbols like *anachronism, disembark, poltroon, ulterior, verisimilitude,* would express the notions implied by those words in simpler language, by a larger number of more elementary symbols. Then every English-speaking person would have in this analytical language a check upon his use of full English; and every foreigner, learning so small a vocabulary very quickly indeed, would have command of a universal tongue.

There were two serious obstacles, the first of which

had already wrecked the hopes of at least one utopian—
Bishop Wilkins. The very few words contemplated must
be strictly harnessed and operated with very severe dis-
criminations; for if its symbols were used as haphazardly
as most words are used, this distilled medium would
soon lose its power to communicate. It was intended to
serve the man in the street, who has not had a prolonged
linguistical or logical or philosophical training, and it
did not seem likely that he was ready for such a discipline. Secondly, suppose you selected your one or
two hundred words and knit them together into a system—how could you make of them a language that
looked or sounded anything like normal English? The
innovation of a definition vocabulary which consisted
of an English-within-English was sure, in any case, to
shock the academics, without their being expected to
swallow any big-music-box-you-push-him-he-shout-you-
pull-him-he-shout sort of thing.

The history of the invention of Basic English is the
story of how these two difficulties were overcome. The
result was a vocabulary—or, as it is best to regard it, a
language system—which, besides being a first-rate mental tool for the intellectual, can greatly benefit the illiter-
ate, as is shown by the citizenship work being done with
adult immigrants to the United States. As regards the
question of whether Basic English is pidgin English—
like all other brands of English, some of it is and some of
it isn't. The summaries of Chief Points at the ends of all
my chapters are written in Basic English, with the addi-

tion, naturally, of such technical terms (mostly nouns) as I have wanted to introduce. The Bible in Basic English, the Basic version of Plato's *Republic,* and L. W. Lockhart's translations from Stevenson and Shaw are examples of good Basic writing. *Good Basic is clear and simple normal English.*

By 1927 C. K. Ogden saw how a definition language could be worked out, with techniques that I shall refer to later. In 1929 he published in *Psyche* a provisional list of words which, with a few small changes, is now Basic English. In 1932 came that famous trio of little books, *The ABC of Basic English, The Basic Words,* and *The Basic Dictionary,* the first two of which explain the system in all its details and provide for any reader anywhere the means of getting fully acquainted with Basic English.

The ABC of Basic English explains what the system is and how to work it. It suggests ways of learning the language and how to teach it to others. Besides being a source book for texts, it is a mine of suggestiveness to anyone interested in the philosophy of language: it describes the functionings of Metaphor, Fictions, and such like expansions of sense, explaining how from their root senses words may focus upon some special sense (e. g. *glass, stamp, judge, card*) or ramify into expanded senses, in the kinds of ways this book has described in connection with shift of meaning. If Basic is to be the hub of our full English, we must know its 850 words inside out. *The Basic Words* lists them all in alphabetical order, shows their central, root senses, and goes into detail on which expanded senses may, and which may not, be used in Basic. It also explains which idioms may be used; for it is important in using an international language not to admit idioms which are too farfetched. *The Basic Dictionary,* instead of containing definitions, consists of suggestions of Basic words which can be substituted for the complex words of normal English. In 1940 was issued a *General Basic English Dictionary,* in which all words and usages are defined in terms of Basic English.

Peace prizes have been given for less important contributions to world betterment than these four books represent. Basic English has made steady progress, especially wherever there has been peace. In the nineteen-thirties, thirty countries were teaching the system, under the guidance of representatives of Mr. Ogden's Orthological Institute in London. Orthological Institutes or Committees sprang up elsewhere, notably in the United States, China, and India. In these and several other countries were published Basic journals and texts especially adapted to local conditions.

It was not till the twenty-first century, however, if we are to believe Mr. Wells, that Basic English was universally adopted as the international auxiliary language!

The Purposes of Basic English

Basic English has three uses. In the first place, it is the most practical and economical international language ever devised. English is already the natural or administrative language of over six hundred million people; millions of others have learned at least some English in foreign schools—so that, although one cannot estimate with certainty, it seems probable that the number of people in the world who are already equipped to understand Basic at a simple level must be nearer a billion than half a billion. Its future, of course, depends on the fate of democracy; but that issue will not be in doubt if democracy does not doubt itself. English-speaking countries control so great a proportion of the decisive industries of radio, motion pictures, the press, aviation, and shipping that English will certainly spread over the globe with greater and greater rapidity. Babel will be overcome by the English language.

Apart from the question of the millions who speak it, English is peculiarly well qualified to form the basis of an international language. It has at least two separate headquarters, which are continually anticipating, checking, and imitating each other. It is the official language of two great commonwealths, and the second language of countries in every continent. Even with its eccentric spelling, and the irregularities of its strong verbs, English is one of the easiest of languages to learn. Half Teutonic and half Latin, it invites those whose language is based upon either Latin or German. Practically its only complications of accidence are found in its verbs and pronouns. (Basic has to keep the pronouns, but has thrown out most of the verbs.) Its nouns and adjectives are not dogged by those problems of "gender, number, and case" which are involved in other European languages.

Simple as English is, Basic English is much simpler still. It has a streamlined vocabulary with which one can say anything one can think of, as far as the plain sense goes. And it has a streamlined grammar, with less than a score of verbs. Since verbs cause most trouble to the student of any European language, this elimination alone is decisive. English had an excellent chance of becoming the universal auxiliary language, and Basic English has turned that chance into a certainty, if civilization is allowed to continue.

The second purpose of Basic English is as the foreign student's first step into fuller English. Many such students, in view of the fact that it is a long job for a foreigner in a foreign country to learn to handle complete English properly, adopt a twofold aim, and set out to learn to write and speak Basic correctly and to read and understand complete English.

For those who mean to tackle the whole language, Basic is the ideal starting point. A total stranger to the 850 words might conceivably learn them all, with their equivalents in his own language, in a day. With such a small vocabulary, eccentric spellings and pronunciations can be thoroughly mastered. Basic is a language which can be "seen at a glance." All the words can be displayed on one side of a sheet of notepaper, together with the basic rules for their manipulation. It is clear that the task of learning this language, a task whose goal can be pinned on the wall and kept in sight throughout the course, can be sifted and graded and arranged with an accuracy and minuteness that could be applied to no complete living language. The names of physical objects and operations will prepare the way for metaphors and Fictions, and very simple sentences will lead up to complex and compound structures.

Basic English is complete in itself; yet it contains all the seeds of full English. The foreign student who proceeds from Basic to complete English is not invading new territory. True, in complete English there are many complex verbs to learn—complex in that each does the work of several words which are simpler semantically; but *send,* in Basic, has already furnished a precedent. *Send* is generally used as shorthand for two simpler verbs. (Which two? How else could we say "I sent him home"?) Jumping from meaning to structural considerations: *seem, seems, seemed* in Basic provides a pattern to guide the learner to form regular verbs from three hundred nouns he has learned in Basic, nouns like *dust, paint, control, work.* (He has already, in Basic, learned to form derivatives such as *worker, working,* and *worked* in its passive use.) As for auxiliaries like *shall, should, can, could,* and *must*—these are new, but they work in sentences just the same as do *will* and *may* (which the student has learned from Basic).

So, merely by its existence, Basic English shows the teacher of full English which step must come after which. In the United States, Basic English is proving itself in an exacting laboratory. The assimilation of aliens is long and arduous work, especially in such states as Massachusetts, where one person in every four is foreign-born. Miss Mary Guyton, State Supervisor of Adult Alien Education in Massachusetts, was one of the first to see that Basic English offered new hope for effectively dealing with her problems. After studying the system in 1935 at C. K. Ogden's Orthological Institute in London, Miss Guyton has ever since taught Basic English to the newcomers to Massachusetts. A certain amount of training in semantic methods is necessary before teachers can switch from the old methods to the new.

The third use of Basic English is as a "sense detector." Anyone who knows it carries in his head a sieve or gauge or measuring rod which he can use to test the quality of any utterance about which he is uncertain. This, the purpose most relevant to us, is being pursued by educators in every state of the Union. (In itself, of course, Basic is not a cure-all: those who use it are interested in orthology as a whole, and they employ it alongside semantic techniques such as are suggested in other chapters.) Pioneers of its use in this country are: Ellen Walpole, of the Children's Studio, New York City, who in applying semantics to the kindergarten level has invented a linguistic training which, among other things, teaches children to read and write accurately and naturally in a far shorter time than is customary; Louis Zahner, of Groton School, a well-known educationist, who has used Basic as one of his instruments for teaching his scholars how language works, and how such knowledge improves one's appreciation of literature; and, on the college and university level, Professor William Albert Upton, of Whittier College, California, who has worked out a combined approach to English and the Social Sciences through orthology and used Basic English as an introduction to problems of classification and abstraction, and Professor Winthrop Tilley, of the University of Connecticut, who uses Basic English as a freshman course in the elements of syntax, composition, and interpretation.

These are teachers who have had several years' experience with Basic. Now its value for schools and colleges is widely recognized by American educationists, and many teachers are using it. These 850 English words (which are listed after this chapter) have been tested and studied as no words in any language were ever studied before. It may be that of some Basic within Basic will be born the "philosophical language" that Bishop Wilkins hoped for!

A Definition Vocabulary

Any three persons who started out to write, respectively, a description of the system of Basic English, a history of its invention, and a manual of instructions for using it would find themselves covering very much the same material. To learn Basic easily one needs to know something of its theory, and one understands that theory twice as well after learning Basic. Readers who mean to follow this chapter's Practice Exercises, and learn how to write and speak Basic—and I urge you to put your semantics to work in this way—should take careful note of this chapter.

After the chapter on Definition, the reader was asked to attach common relevant English words to each of the definition routes which the chapter had discussed. It would be worth while to turn back to page 140, and work through Exercise Two again, because the nuclear vocabulary arrived at in this way represents one of the best ways for a semantician to approach the understanding of Basic English.

Here, arranged under the same twenty-five headings, is about a tenth of the vocabulary of Basic English. Look at these words, see if they bring back the titles of the definition routes, and criticize their inclusion; that is the best way to start learning the 850. (The Basic list never has to be learned by heart.)

1. this that is
2. like same different
3. word language sign say parallel
4. part some of
5. all group unit system
6. opposite cut other
7. scale end
8. space place where in at (and other prepositions)
9. distance from (etc.)
10. old young year month
11. time past present future
12. form round square (etc.)
13. size great small number
14. very much little high low
15. substance material earth water metal (etc.)

16. condition change
17. feeling pleasure pain love (etc.)
18. thought view opinion
19. seeing hearing smelling tasting touching
20. move push pull make put (etc.)
21. behavior way normal strange
22. sex male female man girl (etc.)
23. use purpose work instrument
24. family father mother sister (etc.)
25. law authority government nation judge property

These are all in the Basic English vocabulary. If the reader made a list previously, his list is sure to contain some non-Basic words; but if he chose wisely, all his words are *basic* words. It should not be forgotten that the questions of whether it is possible to invent a self-contained system of basic English words and of whether Basic English represents the best possible selection are two distinct problems at this stage. This point needs to be made here, because the reader who learns Basic may get irritated with it, as one generally does at some stage in the process of learning a language, or indeed of learning any new skill; and it is well for him to see clearly what questions are involved.

It was seen in our examination of contexts and definitions that no one word is indispensable. Specific words can be replaced by more general words—we do this all the time in our conversations with children. To give examples of the kinds of words which Basic found unnecessary (and some which *were* necessary), I will consider the word "man" in some of its connections with the routes of definition. Man is the best thing to take, because he invented our language and every word we use reflects his interests.

Directly symbolized, man is *man* (B.E.), *he* (B.E.), or *she* (B.E.). Like other men, he is *human*. Translated into other languages, he is *hombre, homme, Mann* (etc.) as well as *guy, bloke,* and *chap.* Parts of him are his *head* (B.E.), *heart* (B.E.), *hand* (B.E.), *foot* (B.E.). Considered himself as a part, he is a member of a *family* (B.E.), a *society* (B.E.), and a *nation* (B.E.). Considered in terms of Generalization, he becomes an *animal* (B.E.), a *living* (B.E.) *creature,* and a *thing* (B.E.). His direct opposite, from one point of view, is a *woman* (B.E.), and his opposite on the age scale is a *baby* (B.E.), a *child,* a *boy* (B.E.), or a *girl* (B.E.). With respect to location, he is an *occupant,* a *resident,* and an *inhabitant.* Whatever the name of the place he came from, it could naturally, as a proper name, be used in Basic. His age may stamp him as an *nonagenarian.* History may have made him an *Elizabethan,* in which case Basic would prefer to say that he "was living at the time (or under the rule) of Queen Elizabeth." His shape may entitle us to call him a *brachycephalic,* or even a *Caliban* or a *Quasimodo.* His size may qualify him as a *giant* or a *dwarf* or a *pigmy.* If it is only partially a man, it may be a *sphinx,* a *centaur,* or a *ghost.* Regarded from the material point of view, he is so much *flesh, blood* (B.E.), *skin* (B.E.), *bone* (B.E.), *muscle* (B.E.), *nerve* (B.E.), and so on. He may undergo a change of condition which will oblige us to treat him as a *corpse*. His effect upon his neighbors may qualify him as a *darling* or a *scoundrel*. In their intellectual judgment, he may be a *genius*. His effect upon their eyes may entitle him to call himself a *Negro*. As a result of his or somebody else's actions, he may become an *assassin* or a *victim*. In respect to sex, he or she will be a *male* (B.E.) or a *female* (B.E.), a *man* (B.E.) or a *woman* (B.E.), a *boy* (B.E.) or a *girl* (B.E.). In behavior, he may be a *drunkard;* and his occupation may classify him as an *editor*, a *soldier*, or a *tailor*. In his family, he or she may be a *parent*, a *father* (B.E.) or a *mother* (B.E.), a *brother* (B.E.), a *sister* (B.E.)—and will certainly be a *son* (B.E.) or a *daughter* (B.E.). Legally speaking, he will almost certainly be a *citizen* and at one time or another he may be a *plaintiff* or a *defendant*.

The non-Basic words in this little essay on Man are examples of the sort of word a definition vocabulary can do without. (What would you substitute for these examples?) The theory of definition was an invaluable tool for eliminating words which were not essential. Of course, since Basic was planned for the ordinary purposes of business and science, the linguistic prejudices of ordinary people had to be kept in mind. C. K. Ogden kept three guiding principles before him. First, Basic would have to be practicable for ordinary people and everyday purposes. Second, it must follow the conventions of normal English usage; and *third*, its vocabulary would be limited, and its grammar simplified, to the greatest degree possible in consistency with the first two conditions. In other words, theoretically the way was clear, and the important thing to be done was to make the system practical.

So pros and cons were patiently weighed, all kinds of materials were translated into tentative forms of Basic English, while borderline words were on trial for inclusion or rejection. In hierarchies of Generalization, it was not always the specific words which were rejected. *Parent*, for instance, is not in Basic English—why? Of these four words, one can very conveniently be eliminated (which one?): *fluid, gas, liquid, solid.* Basic made the same choice as you.

As a general rule, Mr. Ogden eliminated words if he could define them in ten Basic words or less. But it would have been bad policy to be hidebound here; and he included in his list two hundred concrete nouns, the names of objects which *could* be defined, or illustrated, but which are handy symbols to have for ordinary conversation, and which make useful, comprehensible metaphors. In Basic one may use the names of concrete things which are not in the 850 list, provided one first introduces the name by pointing to the thing, or by a description or definition or illustration, in writing.

Sixteen Verbs in Basic

In Mr. Ogden's terminology, there are no verbs in Basic English. A verb is a telescoped word, with a complex meaning that implies direction or position as well as action. To disembark is to *get | off | a ship*. Basic keeps such acts and directions apart, and needs the names of only sixteen fundamental acts which function as verbs.

Go is one of the sixteen; and this diagram shows how *go* makes the seven other verbs unnecessary for Basic purposes.

Which seven direction-words in conjunction with *go* will replace those verbs? Prepositions, those operators

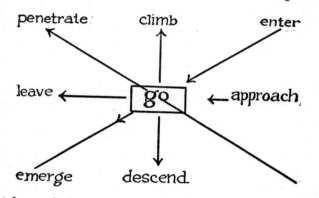

which symbolize positions and directions—*in, out, to, from, with, by,* and others—are getting more and more work to do in standard English; and in Basic their functions must be thoroughly understood. Simple drawings of the relations they symbolize in physical space will establish their root senses, and their metaphorical wanderings, in time (on Tuesday, in May), and among Fictions (under a misapprehension, out of danger), and their idiomatic uses must not be allowed to lose all connection with their root senses. If this sounds complicated, let us put it another way. In speaking Basic, we must use only the 850 simple words, and we must not use even those too slangily or colloquially or idiomatically. Though C. K. Ogden has graded our commonest idioms according to their difficulty, in the last resort the speaker of Basic must judge for himself whether or not to use any given idiom. His decision will base itself upon his particular audience—is it likely to know the idiom? If not, could the meaning be inferred from the context, or from the root senses of the separate words the idiom contains? If he uses it, and finds he has guessed wrong, then he must call upon his techniques of definition.

Naturally, the sixteen verbs combine with other words besides prepositions. One cannot *prepare* in Basic, but one can get ——. You cannot *try* or *attack*, but you can *make* an —— and *make* an ——. You cannot *inform* somebody, but you may give him an ——, or even, more slangily, put him ——. (What are the missing five words?)

Current American uses these sixteen verbs more thoroughly than they are used in other English-speaking countries. Basic English exploits them to the limit: in combination with prepositions, nouns, and adjectives, they can do all the work that verbs have to do.

Why Learn Basic?

There is a mysterious idea afoot that foreigners can learn Basic English very easily, but that those who know English already find Basic very hard to learn. This is erroneous—one can learn to write or talk Basic in a day.

The Basic machinery works a bit stiffly at first, but only the lubrication of practice is necessary.

The English-speaking person who is learning Basic should keep five principles in mind. Firstly, he should have—what this book has tried to present—a fair idea of the theoretical side of Basic and of semantics in general. For Basic is a more "reasonable" language than normal English, and reflection helps more than brute memory in learning it, and the process of learning it constitutes further training in semantic theory. Its connection with the general problems of definition is by now obvious. Our investigation into contexts teaches us to be independent of any particular symbol or symbols. By Metaphor, simple words can be turned to many uses. And, as regards fictions, Basic English shows us how to translate many Fictions into simpler terms, and how to pay close attention to the few hundreds of Fictions in Basic itself. Compared with the sea of ordinary English, Basic represents the firm land of reality.

Secondly, the learner should master Basic English by free writing, or composition, rather than by translation. It is a great temptation to take a paragraph from a book and start off by translating that into Basic, because there is a tangible job to start at. But translation too early may lengthen one's task by months. It is true enough that translation into Basic may be the most important final goal—but this should be delayed until the Basic medium comes freely and easily. The writer should match his Basic symbols against referents, and not against other symbols, which will get in the way of those he is operating.

Thirdly, in his composition exercises he should follow his own interests. If his only interest is in mastering Basic as quickly as possible, one of the best things to do is to describe a picture, or his own immediate surroundings. Then, with his referents right in front of him, he must do what he can with the symbols allowed. If, on the other hand, he is interested in some particular job of communication, these exercises can take the form of minutes of meetings, scientific reports, business communications, or letters to a child or a foreigner. Within five minutes he will find himself better at making himself clear and simple to his colleagues and intelligible to strangers.

Fourthly, another thing to remember if one is taking up Basic in a thorough and fairly leisurely way is to read some Basic writing—the summaries in this book, or other books written in Basic. This helps one to remember words and phrases and to see how ideas are expressed in this medium; and, also, such examples guide one in following the rules of Basic's simplified grammar.

Lastly, do not try to swallow the whole system at a gulp. It takes a day to learn Basic English. Look through the lists of different parts of speech, getting a bird's-eye view of the system as a whole, and then graduate your task, mastering one list at a time. If you start with the verbs, for example, use any nouns and adjectives and other parts of speech that come into your head, and write a few hundred words concentrated on the linguistic feat of using only the sixteen verbs. Then limit yourself further, and further still, until you have shut out every non-Basic word. Follow a method of limitations, either your own or the one suggested after this chapter.

Why learn Basic English? I hope I have shown its main possibilities, but I will try to say briefly why this skill is worth acquiring. To readers with friendly or business relations overseas, I need not emphasize the values of an international language, except to say that such values are bound to increase. At home, Basic is invaluable as a definition vocabulary, and a help in the process of intensive reading which will be dealt with in the last chapter. In itself, the process of learning Basic is a practical course in semantics. In our childhood we learned our language unconsciously, by imitation; and now in learning Basic we have to relearn it, consciously. We can partly judge how valuable this relearning process is by the annoyance we sometimes feel while undergoing it.

After even the first hour at Basic we shall be able to explain situations to strangers and children and foreigners far better than we ever could before. We shall find communication with our friends and families more satisfactory, because the use of Basic gets us into Hobbes's way of regarding words as counters—makes us able to detach ourselves from them and judge our utterances from the other person's point of view. We communicate better because we interpret more fully.

Basic is an immediate step to better writing; it encourages clarity and directness of style. Containing fewer vague and emotive words than our ordinary speech, it makes every sentence say something. The ability to use Basic English might well be demanded of public speakers and writers, as some assurance that they know their craft and are at least not unwitting menaces to the public they address. The discipline of keeping to the rules of Basic gives a sense of "what grammar might be about" and encourages a linguistic conscience.

Perhaps most important of all, Basic writing tends to develop flexibility of style. One's first efforts at Basic are frequently terrible, judged as English—and bad English is bad Basic. After a reasonable time, one's Basic must be criticized by the way it stands up as normal English. The obvious way of saying a certain thing in Basic may ruin the sentence and, therefore, the paragraph. One must try again: there is a way of expressing any thought that is at the same time good Basic and clear, pleasant English.

The use of Basic results in exciting personal discoveries to anyone interested in language. It forces one to consider different ways of expressing more or less the same thought. Such alternatives, crowding before the mind, exercise in us those powers of choice which form the basis of our reasoning and our literary judgment. This, then, is one method by which we can sharpen our wits and help ourselves to value the subtleties of language more sensitively.

Chief Points

Basic English is a language of 850 English words. It was designed for three purposes: as an international language, as a first step to complete English, and as an instrument for getting our thoughts clear. Learning the use of Basic is good training in semantics and a help in the writing of clear English.

Practice Exercises

HOW TO WRITE BASIC ENGLISH

There are people who prefer, after a theoretical bird's-eye view of the system, to write Basic English at once. Perhaps these instructions will help such people, too, though they are addressed to the ordinary learner who prefers to work progressively and thoroughly master one stage before going to the next.

Here, the following different sorts of Basic words will be attended to separately.

1. *Pictured names* (200). These are nouns, the names of separate, picturable, and mostly solid things. Examples: *angle, key, worm.*

2. *Qualities* (150). Adjectives. Examples: *able, awake, young.*

In addition to the 150 Basic qualities, I shall treat as adjectives certain words ending in *-ing* and certain words ending in *-ed.*

(a) *-ing* words. Grammarians have a lot of trouble in classifying these words. I shall deal with them as adjectives unless, like *coming, going, putting,* etc., they belong to the sixteen Basic verbs; or unless, like *learning, reading, writing,* etc., they are listed among the General Names.

Such *-ing* words as Basic permits can be used in every way permissible in ordinary English. One can say: it is a painting, he is painting, he is painting the house, etc.

(b) *-ed* words. These may only be used as adjectives or with the verb *be* (*is, was, are,* etc.). A good rule of thumb question here is to ask oneself if one could substitute for the *-ed* word the adjective *sad,* and still make a grammatical, though not necessarily a sensible, sentence.

> (It is a printed book.
> He printed the book.
> We had printed it.
> The book was printed.

Which of the above four *printed's* are good Basic?)

3. *Adverbs in -ly.* These are adjectives to which the suffix *-ly* has been added. Examples: *angrily, secretly, sweetly.*

4. *General Names* (400). These nouns are mostly the names of Fictions, or of substances or materials; or, to put it another way, the names of things which are *not* picturable. Examples: *account, memory, metal, year.*

5. *Operations* (82). Prepositions, pronouns, adverbs, conjunctions, and other oddments. Examples: *about, some, who, I, almost, yes.*

6. *Verbs and auxiliaries* (18). There are 16 verbs and 2 auxiliaries.

FIRST STEP

The first and most important trick in Basic is to learn to use only 16 verbs and still not neglect the *-ing* and *-ed* possibilities explained above. Write something and check it very carefully for illegal verbs and illicit auxiliaries, and do not leave this step till you can do it well.

1. *Pictured names*   Use all you please.

2. *Qualities*   Any adjectives are permitted, including *-ing* and *-ed* words.

3. *Adverbs in -ly*   Use all such adverbs freely.

4. *General names*   No restrictions.

5. *Operators*   Any operators.

6. *Verbs and auxiliaries*   Use only these verbs: come get give go keep let make put seem take be do have say see send; and these auxiliaries: will may.

The 16 verbs take all their forms and tenses, just as in ordinary English; and *would* and *might*, the past forms of *will* and *may*, can be used.

Warning: Beware of using these words—*can, could, shall, should, must.*

SECOND STEP

Having perfected the first step, now write something using no prepositions, conjunctions, etc. not given below. Do not worry about pronouns, because all of them are in Basic.

1. *Pictured names* No restriction.

2. *Qualities* (including -*ing* and -*ed* words) No restriction.

3. *Adverbs in -ly* No restriction.

4. *General names* No restriction.

5. *Operators* Use only these operators: about across after against among at before between by down from in off on over through to under up with; as for of till than; a the; all any every no other some such; that this; I (me, we, etc.) he (him, it, they, etc.) you (your) who (what, which, whom, etc.); and because but or if though while; how when where why; again ever far forward here near now out still then there together well; almost enough even little much (more, most) not only quite so very; tomorrow yesterday; north south east west; please yes.

Warning: Do not use *that* as a relative pronoun—say "the house *which* Jack made."

Beware of these words, which are not in Basic: *above, also, each, many, too.*

THIRD STEP

When this is mastered, the rest is child's play. The third step is to use only the 400 General Names—concrete nouns may still be used freely.

1. *Pictured names* No restriction.

2. *Qualities* (including -*ing* and -*ed* words) No restriction.

3. *Adverbs in -ly* No restriction.

4. *General names* Use only these general names:

account act addition adjustment advertisement agreement air amount amusement animal answer apparatus approval argument art attack attempt attention attraction authority;

back balance base behavior belief birth bit bite blood blow body brass bread breath brother building burn burst business butter;

canvas care cause chalk chance change cloth coal color comfort committee company comparison competition condition connection control cook copper copy cork cotton cough country cover crack credit crime crush cry current curve;

damage danger daughter day death debt decision degree design desire destruction detail development digestion direction discovery discussion disease disgust distance distribution division doubt drink driving dust;

earth edge education effect end error event example exchange existence expansion experience expert;

fact fall family father fear feeling fiction field fight fire flame flight flower fold food force form friend front fruit;

glass gold government grain grass grip group growth guide;

harbor harmony hate hearing heat help history hole hope hour humor;

ice idea impulse increase industry ink insect instrument insurance interest invention iron;

jelly join journey judge jump;

kick kiss knowledge;

land language laugh law lead learning leather letter level lift light limit linen liquid list look loss love;

machine man manager mark market mass meal measure meat meeting memory metal middle milk mind mine minute mist money month morning mother motion mountain move music;

name nation need news night noise note number;

observation offer oil operation opinion order organization ornament owner;

page pain paint paper part paste payment peace person place plant play pleasure point poison polish porter position powder power price print process produce profit property prose protest pull punishment purpose push;

quality question;

rain range rate ray reaction reading reason record regret relation religion representative request respect rest reward rhythm rice river road roll room rub rule run;

salt sand scale science sea seat secretary selection self sense servant sex shade shake shame shock side sign silk silver sister size sky sleep slip slope smash smell smile smoke sneeze snow soap society son song sort sound soup space stage start statement steam steel step stitch stone stop story stretch structure substance sugar suggestion summer support surprise swim system;

talk taste tax teaching tendency test theory thing thought

thunder time tin top touch trade transport trick trouble turn twist;

unit use;

value verse vessel view voice;

walk war wash waste water wave wax way weather week weight wind wine winter woman wood wool word work wound writing;

year.

Note on -er words: Words like *attacker, painter, printer, writer* may be formed from the words in the list above, if such derivatives exist in ordinary English.

5. and 6. Operators, verbs, and auxiliaries in strict Basic.

FOURTH STEP

1. *Pictured names*   No restriction.

2. *Qualities*   Use only these adjectives:

able acid angry automatic awake;

bad beautiful bent bitter black blue boiling bright broken brown;

certain cheap chemical chief clean clear cold common complete complex conscious cruel cut;

dark dead dear deep delicate dependent different dirty dry;

early elastic electric equal;

false fat feeble female fertile first fixed flat foolish free frequent full future;

general good great green gray;

hanging happy hard healthy high hollow;

ill important;

kind;

last late left like living long loose loud low;

male married material medical military mixed;

narrow natural necessary new normal;

old open opposite;

parallel past physical political poor possible present private probable public;

quick quiet;

ready red regular responsible right rough round;

sad safe same second separate serious sharp short shut simple slow small smooth soft solid special sticky stiff straight strange strong sudden sweet;

tall thick thin tight tired true;

violent;

waiting warm wet white wide wise wrong;

yellow young.

Use comparatives and superlatives—*more* tired, *most* tired, sadd*er*, sadd*est*—as in ordinary English.

Use *un-* (meaning *not*) before any adjective that takes it in ordinary English.

3. *Adverbs in -ly*   Use only such *-ly* adverbs as are formed from the adjectives listed above.

4., 5., and 6. General Names, operators, verbs, and auxiliaries in strict Basic.

FIFTH STEP

1. *Pictured names*   Use only those names of things that can be pictured:

angle ant apple arch arm army;

baby bag ball band basin basket bath bed bee bell berry
bird blade board boat bone book boot bottle box boy
brain brake branch brick bridge brush bucket bulb
button;

cake camera card carriage cart cat chain cheese chest
chin church circle clock cloud coat collar comb cord
cow cup curtain cushion;

dog door drain drawer dress drop;

ear egg engine eye;

face farm feather finger fish flag floor fly foot fork fowl
frame;

garden girl glove goat gun;

hair hammer hand hat head heart hook horn horse hospital house;

island;

jewel;

kettle key knee knife knot;

leaf leg library line lip lock;

map match monkey moon mouth muscle;

nail neck needle nerve net nose nut;

office orange oven;

parcel pen pencil picture pig pin pipe plane plate plow
pocket pot potato prison pump;

rail rat receipt ring rod roof root;

sail school scissors screw seed sheep shelf ship shirt shoe
skin skirt snake sock spade sponge spoon spring square
stamp star station stem stick stocking stomach store
street sun;

table tail thread throat thumb ticket toe tongue tooth
town train tray tree trousers;
umbrella;
wall watch wheel whip whistle window wing wire worm.

This is now strict Basic English; and -er, -ing, and
-ed words may now be used only if they are formed from
Basic nouns. (Thus, *planting* and *framing* are in Basic
but *roping* and *starching* are not, because *rope* and
starch are not.)

A SUMMARY OF POINTS TO REMEMBER

1. Start writing Basic before trying to memorize all
the details about its use. If uncertain about any point
not mentioned in this book, study examples in books
mentioned in this chapter or write for information to
The Orthological Committee, Cambridge, Massachusetts, or the Orthological Institute, London, England. I
am indebted to these institutions for permission to use
these Basic materials, which should not be reproduced
without their permission.

2. Words like paint*er*, paint*ing*, paint*ed* may be used
in Basic if their elementary form is in the vocabulary;
but -*ed* words must not be used as "finite verbs."

3. All the pronouns of English are in Basic; but *that*
should not be used as a relative pronoun.

4. Compound nouns may be formed from Basic words:
that is, a noun may be used as an adjective.

5. Beware of forming derivatives which are not al-

lowed in Basic. The suffixes *-y, -ful, -less, -ness* are not permissible. (*Un-* is the only prefix in Basic, and the only suffixes are *-er, -ing, -ed; -er, -est; -ly.*)

6. Numbers, dates, currency, weights, and measures, and certain words which are used almost universally, can be used in Basic in their normal English form.

7. Any nouns or adjectives needed for special purposes can be introduced into Basic writing or conversation, if they are first defined.

8. Write short, ten-to-twelve-word sentences until the whole system of Basic comes easily.

9. Finally, when you know the system, judge your Basic by the way it stands up as normal English. Bad English is bad Basic!

10. Learning Basic will help you in learning foreign languages.

Alphabetic List of the Words of Basic English

a able about account acid across act addition adjustment advertisement after again against agreement air all almost among amount amusement and angle angry animal answer ant any apparatus apple approval arch argument arm army art as at attack attempt attention attraction authority automatic awake

baby back bad bag balance ball band base basin basket bath be beautiful because bed bee before behavior belief bell bent berry between bird birth bit bite bitter black blade blood blow blue board boat body boiling bone book boot bottle box boy brain brake branch brass bread breath brick bridge bright broken brother brown brush bucket building bulb burn burst business but butter button by

cake camera canvas card care carriage cart cat cause certain chain chalk chance change cheap cheese chemical chest chief chin church circle clean clear clock cloth cloud coal coat cold collar color comb come comfort committee common company comparison competition complete complex condition connection conscious control cook copper copy cord cork cotton cough country cover cow crack credit crime cruel crush cry cup current curtain curve cushion cut

damage danger dark daughter day dead dear death debt decision deep degree delicate dependent design desire destruction detail development different digestion direction dirty discovery discussion disease disgust distance distribution division do dog door doubt down drain drawer dress drink driving drop dry dust

ear early earth east edge education effect egg elastic electric end engine enough equal error even event ever every example exchange existence expansion experience expert eye

face fact fall false family far farm fat father fear feather feeble feeling female fertile fiction field fight finger fire

first fish fixed flag flame flat flight floor flower fly fold
food foolish foot for force fork form forward fowl
frame free frequent friend from front fruit full future

garden general get girl give glass glove go goat gold
good government grain grass gray great green grip
group growth guide gun

hair hammer hand hanging happy harbor hard harmony
hat hate have he (it, they, etc.) head healthy hearing
heart heat help here high history hole hollow hook
hope horn horse hospital hour house how humor

I (us, our, etc.) ice idea if ill important impulse increase
industry ink insect instrument insurance interest invention iron island

jelly jewel join journey judge jump

keep kettle key kick kind kiss knee knife knot knowledge

land language last late laugh law lead leaf learning
leather left leg let letter level library lift light like limit
line linen lip liquid list little living lock long look loose
loss loud love low

machine make male man manager map mark market
married mass match material may (might) meal measure meat medical meeting memory metal middle mili-

tary milk mind mine minute mist mixed money monkey month moon morning mother motion mountain
mouth move much (more, etc.) music muscle

nail name narrow nation natural near necessary neck
need needle nerve net new news night no noise normal
north nose not note now number nut

observation of off offer office oil old on only open operation opinion opposite or orange order organization
ornament other out oven over owner

page pain paint paper parallel parcel part past paste payment peace pen pencil person physical picture pig pin
pipe place plane plant plate play please pleasure plow
pocket point poison polish political poor porter position possible pot potato powder power present price
print prison private probable process produce profit
property prose protest public pull pump punishment
purpose push put

quality question quick quiet quite

rail rain range rat rate ray reaction reading ready reason
receipt record red regret regular relation religion representative request respect responsible rest reward
rhythm rice right ring river road rod roll roof room
root rough round rub rule run

sad safe sail salt same sand say scale school science scissors screw sea seat second secret secretary see seed
seem selection self send sense separate serious servant
sex shade shake shame sharp sheep shelf ship shirt
shock shoe short shut side sign silk silver simple sister
size skin skirt sky sleep slip slope slow small smash
smell smile smoke smooth snake sneeze snow so soap
society sock soft solid some son song sort sound soup
south space spade special sponge spoon spring square
stage stamp star start statement station steam steel
stem step stick sticky stiff still stitch stocking stomach
stone stop store story straight strange street stretch
strong structure substance such sudden sugar suggestion summer sun support surprise sweet swim system

table tail take talk tall taste tax teaching tendency test
than that the then theory there thick thin thing this
though thought thread throat through thumb thunder
ticket tight till time tin tired to toe together tomorrow
tongue tooth top touch town trade train transport tray
tree trick trouble trousers true turn twist

umbrella under unit up use

value verse very vessel view violent voice

waiting walk wall war warm wash waste watch water
wave wax way weather week weight well west wet

wheel when where while whip whistle white who (what, which, etc.) why wide will (would) wind window wine wing winter wire wise with woman wood wool word work worm wound writing wrong

year yellow yes yesterday you (your) young

10

INTENSIVE READING:
THE VALUE OF PARAPHRASE

*No, Socrates, the limit of such a discussion, for a
wise man, is all his days.*
Glaucon, *in* PLATO's *Republic, Book 5.*

LISTS of best books mean nothing vital to the average
reader, and there are no rules of thumb or charts
of instructions on what to do with "a book" in general
that cannot be improved upon by the average reader
himself, individually. To read a book well is to ask the
right questions about it; and it seems obvious that the
same prescribed questions will not do every time. The
right questions are those which arise from the special nature of the particular book or which grow out of the one
reader's own mind.

The trouble is that we tend to regard reading and living as two separate activities, rather in conflict with
each other. The traditional eulogy of books never gets
far away from their ancient recommendation as a recipe
for "holdinge ye olde menn from ye chimenee cornere."
Yet we know that language is concentrated living, and
books consist of language concentrated. The laws of living, if there are any, are as applicable to books as to
anything else. And the man in the street who sees

that reading adds to his social life—rather than competes with it—will resent devoting a bit of toil to his reading no more than he resents spending a little labor on his garden or dancing or fishing or bridge. What books should he read? He is the best judge of that. He will presumably choose a book which interests him, which seems worth spending time on, and which makes demands on him. Something, perhaps, which is slightly above his reach. Such a book may prove a better tonic than most forms of work or recreation, especially for men and women whose daily business has little to do with reading or writing.

The great thing, though, is for the reader to interpret the verb *read* in its pregnant sense and really read his book, and read its most important parts intensively. Good reading leads to the choice of better books, and better books demand better reading, and so on, with an infinite reciprocity. But a person must begin from where he is, on his own type of book. This may well be a novel: a good novel generously rewards the intensive rereading of its crucial passages. Such reading, of course, is not called for by the kind of fiction which depends for its appeal upon the reader's eagerness to know what happened next.

This chapter, then, takes the position that we all read enough, but not deeply enough. It assumes a reader who has a book in which he is interested, who is ready to give it a preliminary reading to get the lay of the land and then go back and read intensively certain passages which seem especially significant. They are significant in our technical sense—they are signs, pointers to all the rest of the book. In reading them thoroughly, we read the whole book; and all our semantic knowledge, without necessarily coming out into the open, will be at work, helping us to understand the author's meaning.

The Delayed Response

Our modern ways of living tend to make us judge the efficiency of a man's thinking by the speed with which he comes to a decision. The ideal thinker, in this view, is the executive who sits at a desk and sends monosyllabic barks into nine telephones practically simultaneously. In business, in war, and in other matters-of-life-and-death we sometimes have to make up our minds quickly if we are to survive; but, at other times, instantaneous decisions are not the most efficient. Those central decisions which guide our conduct toward ourselves and the universe we have a lifetime to make, and, as Glaucon points out to Socrates, it is shockingly inefficient to "solve" such problems too quickly.

Our reading is a great influence in the development of these decisions, and deserves to be taken very seriously. Any technique for improved reading is good if it enables one to react more fully to what the author is saying. This is not a platitude—we too often react to our own opinions without giving the author a chance; and in training ourselves to be better readers our principal

need will always be to find ways of training ourselves
to postpone our decision until we understand the issue
to be decided.

At one stage in Pavlov's experiments, when he was
waiting thirty seconds between ringing the bell and offering the food, his dog learned to relax for almost that time
before letting his mouth water. The dog learned more
efficient behavior. Any ways we can discover of delay-
ing our final reaction until communication is complete
will improve our behavior as readers. I am not advocat-
ing a period of doglike, unconscious stupor between
perusal and judgment!

A very competent reviewer, in his notice of M. Jules
Romains's *Seven Mysteries of Europe,* told us that Romains made "the flat statement, unqualified and unsup-
ported, that at the time of the German attack on Belgium
last May, King Leopold 'had pretended to resist and
appealed to the Anglo-French armies to draw them into
the trap.'" I cannot find that Romains did make this
flat statement; but the reviewer continued, "What's the
use of examining M. Romains further, or of taking anything he says with any seriousness at all?" Luckily most
of us are not called upon to do our reading at reviewing
speed, but we all run the risk of making similarly drastic
judgments at the drop of a hat. Like Alexander, we cut
the Gordian knot—and Lewis Mumford has pointed out
that this was not very clever of Alexander: he was simply
being a Hun before his time.

Our interpretation of an utterance may be said to fall

into three stages: what we think it might mean, what we think it does mean, what we think of it. Our effectiveness at the second stage depends entirely upon our success with the first, and the last stage depends upon the second. I have nothing to say about the last stage—that is the reader's own business. But to explain the first two, in an effort to pin down specimens in the act, as it were, of being read intensively, I chose three passages and asked people to read them according to my instructions.

Much of the rest of this chapter consists of a dramatization of the process of reading these passages. I have recorded what happened in the minds of my friends. All this will be very dull for the present reader if he simply follows it as if it were a narrative; but interesting, I think, if he himself takes part in the experiment. Read the passages intensively yourself, by following the instructions; and, besides doing this work yourself, study the way other people read the passages, and mentally answer their questions as well as your own; and, finally, since this reading method must for expository purposes be formalized here, adapt it to your own need or taste.

Questions

The reader is ready to study a key passage from his book. He goes through it alertly, making a note of every question or doubt or problem that could possibly arise in anybody's mind, either from the entire drift of the passage as a whole or from any of its details. Do not at first condemn any question because it seems silly: the reasons why a question is silly—because it is quite off the point, or needs information which is not available, or is just one of those questions that have no answer—all cast light upon the author's meaning and define it in more than one sense of that overworked word. Nobody will frame silly questions on purpose. As for sensible ones, the better the reader, the longer this first stage takes—the more difficulties he thinks of.

So give my three passages the works, in the ways suggested, and go over the ideas of other readers, too. Here is the first passage.

A

1. Every civilized person desires peace. 2. This argument indeed is addressed only to those who believe in peace and know that most of the things men of good will hold dear can be achieved only in a state of peace: we are opposed to "those hirelings in the court, the camp, and the university who would forever depress mental and prolong corporeal war." 3. Those who believe that war is a permanent attribute of human life, like eating, rather than an obsolete cultural form, like cannibalism, need read no further; this book is not for them.

4. But peace is neither a state of political Nirvana nor a moral vacuum: no state of peace is tolerable in which the savage and the debased have the upper hand over the rest of humanity; on the contrary, the real problem of peace is to weld force to humane purposes and to use it for humane ends. 5. But there are higher aims, all decent men agree, than merely preserving human life or fending off death; peace in that purely negative sense is indeed worthy of the soldier's ancient contempt.

Every civilized person desires peace.

Does the author assume that *civilized* means the same
to everyone? Or has he previously said what he means
by *civilized?* Or is he here saying "this is what I mean by
that word"? What does he mean by it? On what basis do
we normally say that a person is civilized? What sorts
of people are civilized—who is, for instance? Would a
man who eats with his hat on be certain to be among
the *un*civilized, here? Would a person with scientific
training be civilized, unquestionably? Can we be wholly
civilized if we are not working to make the whole world
more civilized? Is every person uncivilized who does
not desire peace? Does this author mean to use *civilized*
with personal, or social, implications—or both?

And what is *peace?* Could it be peace of mind? Are
there not different sorts of peace? What context or setting is uppermost here—is it peace in the home—in the
community—in the nation—in the world? Could *peace*
ever be a polite name for stagnation, or enslavement,
or ruin?

*This argument indeed is addressed only to those who
believe in peace and know that most of the things men
of good will hold dear can be achieved only in a state of
peace: we are opposed to "those hirelings in the court,
the camp, and the university who would forever depress
mental and prolong corporeal war."*

How can this be an *argument,* if the author addresses only those who agree with him? Or is it that he takes for granted an abstract love for a rather vague peace in general, but wants to disentangle some of the implications behind a platitude? What motive can he have in refusing to address a certain portion of the public? Or is he simply saying that the virtues of peace as against war, other things being equal, seem so obvious that he is not interested to discuss them?

What does one do when one *believes in* peace—believe that it exists—that it is a good thing—that it is a possibility?

Who are these *men of good will*—men like the author? All the men of whom the author approves? Does the phrase mean men with an active will to do good? Who, for example, is a man of good will? What are half a dozen of the things that men of good will hold dear? Are such things necessarily the most desirable things for us, biologically, psychologically, spiritually?

Can a *state of peace* be imposed by force?

Why quote without giving the author of the quotation? What is the emotional effect of this quotation? Who are such hirelings? What is the implication of the word *hireling*—a person who would do anything for money or advancement or security? Do *camp* and *court* stand for professional military officers and politicians? Are all such people, together with professors, condemned here? Is to *depress mental war* to put an end to the free exchange of ideas? Why should men who believe in war for its own sake want to stop people from thinking freely?

Have wars ever resulted in reforms and beneficial inventions? Is war sometimes necessary, to keep what civilization we have?

Those who believe that war is a permanent attribute of human life, like eating, rather than an obsolete cultural form, like cannibalism, need read no further; this book is not for them.

Is cannibalism obsolete in the sense that nobody eats human flesh anywhere? If it still is practiced in obscure corners of the earth would that fact destroy this particular argument? Does he mean obsolete in civilized countries? And does he define civilized countries as those whose citizens disapprove of war and cannibalism?

If war is sometimes necessary, could the same thing conceivably be said of cannibalism?

By "war" the author obviously means corporeal war, does he not?

Is not "need read no further" rather a dramatic gesture? Is it simply a way of saying that there may be such people, but he is not concerned with them? Why not —because they are not civilized, or because argument is hopeless in their case?

But peace is neither a political Nirvana nor a moral vacuum: no state of peace is tolerable in which the savage and the debased have the upper hand over the rest of humanity; on the contrary, the real problem of peace is to weld force to humane purposes and to use it for humane ends.

Is the author not changing his definition of *peace* here? Is this a refined sense of the word? What is the distinction between a political Nirvana and a moral vacuum? Would a political Nirvana be a sort of Buddhist heaven, in which there was not only no political activity, but no activity of any sort—only harmony and rest? Is a moral vacuum a condition in which questions of right and wrong are irrelevant? Is the author playing this trick upon us—saying that those people of whom he approves are civilized, men of good will, tolerable, humane, higher, and decent men; and those he dislikes are savage, debased, obsolete, and hirelings?

What are the implications of *humane*—kind, desiring not to give pain, working for the general well-being of society? What is the function of *weld* here? Does he mean we must not use force except as something inseparable from idealistic purposes? Is *tolerable* an emotive word? Does it imply tolerable to the author—to all civilized persons?

But there are higher aims, all decent men agree, than merely preserving human life or fending off death: peace in that purely negative sense is indeed worthy of the soldier's ancient contempt.

But is generally used to convey something like "however, in contrast to what I have just said, I will now say that . . ."; but does it mean that here?

Obviously *higher* is used metaphorically; could we

give examples of high aims and low aims, and with their help define this property of being higher? Could we name some generally accepted high aims? Are all decent men civilized men—and vice versa? In other words, are the *decent men* our old friends the civilized persons, etc? If this were the case, and such words were used as synonyms, is not this device sometimes helpful and necessary—like expressing the number 18 as 9 times 2 as well as 18 times 1 and 3 times 6? Does each of the words in question make a special contribution of its own?

Can anything be more important than saving human life? Are any conditions so bad that one would die rather than suffer them? Would the fact that decent men were ready to die prevent such conditions from becoming possible?

Is not *worthy* another approval-word? And *ancient* is somewhat poetical—does it express the idea that soldiers from all time have had a low opinion of a certain sort of peace?

Commenting on the passage as a whole, my friends asked such questions as these:

Should it not be considered as an expression of the author's feelings as well as a statement of his opinions? Does it consist of a series of definitions of *peace* and *civilized*, as if the author were saying: "Let us examine these words *peace* and *civilized*, as they are commonly used, and also as they must be used if they are to be reconciled"?

B

1. Science is deeply skeptical of the threefold approach to the external world. 2. It asserts that matter, when tracked down in the laboratory to a point at which it disappears even from the discerning eye of the microscope, is reducible to a formula which equates it with events; and it notes that an object, so far as our description of it goes, is nothing but a complex of sense-impressions which, taken by themselves, might be referred to adjectivally. 3. Strip an object of its qualities and language balks. 4. But language, except when terms have been redefined and fitted into a system by specialists, is not built up at the scientist's level.

5. Nor is it likely that it would be as efficient a medium for communication for everyday purposes if this had been the case. 6. It is very much an *ad hoc* affair, and if the orthologist forgets this and treats language as though it had resulted from a scientific approach he is likely to go astray. 7. It is most improbable that a study of grammatical logic will shed any light on the nature of existence.

Science is deeply skeptical of the threefold approach to the external world.

Who is this *science?* What is the *threefold approach?* And what sorts of approach are indicated—ways of thinking about, ways of understanding, ways of dealing with, ways of acting toward? All of these? Some—or something different?

External as opposed to what—to ourselves, to thoughts and feelings? Are the workings of the mind excluded? If so, because they are not approached by the three-way method—or because scientists would have no objection to such a method being used in such matters? Would logic be excluded from the external world?

It asserts that matter, when tracked down in the laboratory to a point at which it disappears even from the discerning eye of the microscope, is reducible to a formula which equates it with events; and it notes that an object, so far as our description of it goes, is nothing but a complex of sense-impressions which, taken by themselves, might be referred to adjectively.

Does the first *it* refer to science, or to the threefold approach? Could we substitute for it "objective fact, according to most scientists of authority"? Who are such scientists?

How does one *track down* matter—does this simply mean examining, with microscopes, as minutely as possible? What other kinds of things are done to track down matter?

Does *matter* mean the *external world?* How can matter be reduced to a formula? Is not every name we give to matter some sort of a formula?

What does *equates* mean? Does this imply that those external objects, etc., which, on the level of our sense-impressions, seem to be things and substances become, on the scientist's level, series of events?

Is it not possible to refer to any thing by nouns *or* by adjectives, according to our taste or purpose?

Does this mean that it is *best* to refer to such objects adjectively—to say of a chair, for instance, that it is hardish, brownish, mahoganyish, and chairish? But even so, would not such adjectives be of different kinds? Is there nothing in an object apart from our interpretation of it? *Strip an object of its qualities and language balks.*

Strip an object of its qualities and one could still call it a chair, could one not? Or is being-a-chair just one of the chair's qualities? Can it be that the name *chair* involves certain qualities of shape, function, and so on without which it could not be called a chair? Or is the author still talking about the microscopic level? If so, is an adjective any better than a noun for referring to an event?

Whenever I think of *chair* in general, of the type *chair,* I strip the referent of many of its qualities, do I not? How does language *balk?*

But language, except when terms have been redefined and fitted into a system by specialists, is not built up at the scientist's level.

Which sciences have the most exact classification and the least ambiguous terminology? Psychology—economics—physics—mechanics—mathematics? Does their exactness depend upon their subject matter?

Does this sentence say that our ordinary use of words is not as precise as the scientist needs for his purposes? *Nor is it likely that it would be as efficient a medium for communication for everyday purposes if this had been the case.*

Is it certain that our language was not constructed scientifically? Does this sentence mean that ordinarily we do not talk with scientific precision? Would we become tongue-tied if we tried to? Could not ordinary conversation, though demanding a flexibility and a breadth of range greater than specialist subjects call for, be cultivated as both an art and a science?

It is very much an ad hoc *affair, and if the orthologist forgets this and treats language as though it had resulted from a scientific approach he is likely to go astray.*

Does *ad hoc* mean pragmatic? Does this mean that language has been built up by being patched and improvised for special immediate purposes?

Who is the orthologist—the linguistic scientist? Does this imply that the orthologist should not treat language scientifically?

It is most improbable that a study of grammatical logic will shed any light on the nature of existence.

What is grammatical logic—the attempt to discover such things as the laws of sentence structure? Surely such a study might shed light on the nature of human existence? What sort of existence is meant—life, the external world, reality as opposed to appearance?

Does it not seem clear that "the threefold approach" is our habit, derived from our language, of regarding the world as composed of things, qualities, and events? Does it say that we cannot expect our language to mirror the latest findings of scientists? And that, on the other hand, when we discuss scientific matters in normal conversation, we are obliged to describe those findings in the language we inherit, unsuitable though that may be?

C

1. Psychiatry as I had known it before had been barren of interest and hopeless in outlook despite my great interest in mental processes, an interest which I seemed to have displayed throughout my college and university years. 2. To be sure, there had been plenty to do in the state hospital, neuropathologically and psychiatrically, but it had all come down to a few formulas, this or that form of dementia praecox, or this or that form of manic-depressive insanity, etc. 3. In Burgholzli it was quite different: instead of diagnosing this or that form of dementia praecox, which could be done at sight after a little experience, we focused our interest on the particular expressions of the patient. 4. Instead of simply saying that the patient had hallucinations of hearing, we wished to know why he heard these particular voices, for, following Freud, we invariably found that these particular hallucinations could be perceived only by this particular patient. 5. They told the struggles of his wrecked mental life.

6. Jung was at that time the most ardent Freudian. 7. Had I been better acquainted with the Freudian mechanisms, I could have foretold what was to happen a few years later. 8. But now Jung brooked no disagreement with Freud's views; impulsive and bright, he refused to see the other side. 9. Anyone who dared doubt what was certainly then new and revolutionary immediately aroused his anger. 10. Nevertheless, psychoanalysis owes him much, his enthusiasm and brilliance soon placed him at the forefront of the battle line. 11. He was my first, and, I might say, my most vehement teacher. 12. I read the *Traumdeutung* under his guidance.

Barren of interest and hopeless in outlook.

Does the author mean "as far as I was concerned," or not?

Neuropathologically and psychiatrically.

What is this distinction, if it is meant to be one? Are these words concerned with diseases of the nerves and of the mind respectively? How can we find out to what extent it is useful to make such a distinction?

Expressions.

Utterances, symptoms, manifestations?

Hallucinations . . . voices.

Are hallucinations of hearing necessarily voices?

Perceived.

In what sense are these hallucinations perceived? Is there an implication that other sufferers could perceive them as well if they chose to?

Struggles.

Did these struggles wreck the mental life? Then did they cease?

Freudian.

A believer in Freud? An active follower of Freud? An authority on Freud?

Mechanisms.

Are these mechanisms the unconscious directives of mental processes?

Impulsive and bright.

Does the author imply that such people naturally find it hard to see the other point of view?

New and revolutionary.

Was Jung angry when people refused to accept *all* revolutionary ideas?

Traumdeutung.

Who wrote this book? What is its English title?

Why will the normal reader find this passage more difficult than the other two to consider out of its context? How much of a knowledge of its technical terms is essential?

Paraphrase and Comparison

The reader's next task is to decide what the author has said. Not what he, the reader, would say on that subject, or what the writer ought to have said—but to get a faithful reflection of the ideas and sentiments of the original. If the author says nothing that amounts to anything, or if he turns out to be hopelessly confused, ambiguous, or contradictory, it may occasionally be worth while to write a detailed report on his failure; but usually the best remedy is the choice of a better book. Here I take for granted a piece of writing which hangs together.

This second stage represents the most important part of the reading process. The first stage consists of orientation toward this central task, and the third, that of critical judgment, of reorientation after it. The final criticism, demanding modification of one's previous outlook, may take some time to develop.

But how can we "decide what the author has said"?

That is what we always try to do when we read, is it not? We can set ourselves a task which automatically will make us attend to the author's meaning more closely than we usually do. The ancient and modern problem of finding another's referents underlies all communication, however complex or however elementary. It is the same problem that was illustrated by an Associated Press item from Canton, Ohio, which appeared in American newspapers in November, 1940.

Deputy Clerk T. H. Depew was registering an alien who could neither read nor write.

"Put your X right there," he said, indicating the dotted line with an index finger.

"Oh, ya, sure," said the eager registrant, and quickly drew an X on Depew's fingernail.

I wonder what Mr. Depew did next. Did he laugh, or say "That's wrong," and so convince the newcomer that he had mistaken the symbol for the referent and make him rack his brains until he found the right referent? Or did Mr. Depew take a different symbol, like a pencil, or a different finger, or a stick, and so by diverse symbolization point the way to the appropriate referent? The same kinds of mistake occur at all levels of our intellectual life, and we are ceaselessly called upon to expand our symbols, to define, to paraphrase.

That is the thing to do with a passage we are reading intensively. Readers who know some French, German,

Italian, Spanish, or any other foreign language will remember how much one can learn from an interesting passage in the process of translating it from one language into another. Any kind of translation is very valuable, because it makes us think very actively about the author's meaning. It forces us to change the order of words, to expand—by some sort of definition—symbols which have no equivalents in the new medium, and all this makes us probe for the author's referents. Word-by-word translation is never completely possible, and is attempted only by translators who do not know the new medium and are translating in order to learn it—a calamitous situation!

When the translation is finished, it will never be "perfect," for obvious reasons. It is a gauge by which to judge the original; by comparison of the two we have more chance of discovering what the original almost said, or might have said, or does not quite make clear whether it is saying or not. And all this gets us much nearer to knowing what he did say, to the point of perfect communication—which, of course, is never achieved, any more than we can ever make one pencil exactly the same length as another.

So any sort of translation, of passages which are worth translating, is very profitable. The comparison of two versions of the same idea refines our faculties for discriminating between shades of sense and nuances of feeling. The merits of any particular translation provide only a rough measure of the values obtained, which come from the processes of translation and comparison.

For those who have only one language, *paraphrase*—expressing the same ideas in different English words—serves a similar purpose. But better still is *analytical paraphrase,* which plunges one more deeply into the meaning of the original. By analytical paraphrase I mean translating the passage into Basic English; but some people may prefer just using the Basic vocabulary as a list of words instead of as a system, or even be content to put the passage into "simpler words." The natural way of doing this last is to underline those words which produced questions in the first stage of reading and replace them by definitions. I recommend strict Basic English; it takes a little trouble at first, but when you have it you have it. But for the rest of the discussion the reader may change "Basic English" into "the definition vocabulary" if he pleases.

Without repeating details of theory which previous chapters have fully explored, I will illustrate the difference between analytical paraphrase and the other kinds of paraphrase or translation. Many of the difficulties of a passage can be glossed over by old-fashioned ways of paraphrasing into normal English or translating into a different language. Suppose, for some reason, one were tackling the sentence: "The king justified the confiscation." Translating this into French, the same words would serve: *Le roi justifia la confiscation.* If we were paraphrasing into other English words, we could say, "The monarch vindicated the appropriation." Neither of these alternatives demands much of an insight into the situation. Basic would not let us off so lightly. We would be obliged to look at the context before we could write an interpretation, and would find out that in Voltaire's original story, from which the above sentence in French is taken, certain subjects are complaining because the king has ordered all copies of a certain set of books to be destroyed. In reply to their protest, "the king said that his servants had been right in taking those books from their owners," or "the king gave reasons in support of his orders," or "the king said that in his opinion he had been wise to give such orders." (I emphasize that this is given as an example, not as an argument in itself.) Translating into Basic English makes it necessary to break up a situation into its elements; and to do this one must know what those elements are. There is no necessity here to distinguish between the insight that comes from reflection alone and that which results from additional information obtained from a friend or a dictionary or a reference book or a knowledge of the author's life. Our ordinary reading is not done under examination conditions and it needs all the help it can get.

The present reader will soon be asked to turn back to the three passages and translate them into Basic English. It might be said that isolated passages like these are not a fair task, and in a way this is true. The reader deals best with passages of his own choice, taken from books which he has selected for himself. A real job of intensive reading calls for a thorough knowledge of the passage's context—of the rest of the book and of the author. But "unknown" passages have their own peculiar advantages. These passages, and the others which follow at the end of the chapter, can be a mental tonic because the reader will be free of the prejudices he would feel if he knew the names of their authors; and this will help him to discover what he really thinks on certain important matters. The purpose of this chapter is to demonstrate a method and to invite the reader to consider how much of it he can use, and in what form; and an essential part of this method is the choice of subject matter which is not trivial.

Basic English will give its best service as an instrument of analysis if the translator guards against four dangers. The first is the danger of writing too soon, before weighing all the possibilities of the passage—the danger of not seeing all the angles. Basic itself forces us to see many of them because of its small vocabulary: in fact, careful as we may be to list every conceivable problem beforehand, the process of finding Basic equivalents is certain to uncover difficulties of which we had not thought. But even Basic can gloss over some difficulties. Words like *belief, interest, outlook, peace,* and *science,* for example, which are Basic words, are capable of causing trouble, as we have seen in the passages under discussion. A good analytical paraphrase will expand such words where necessary; they are fewer in Basic, and we get to know their journeyings better.

The second danger to avoid is the mistake of invariably following the sentence-patterns of the original. Sometimes it is best to turn a sentence the other way round, or inside out. Sometimes it is best to split it into several sentences.

The third danger often accompanies the second: Basic often invites us to get too vague or too general. It is a great temptation to call "the archaeologist" simply "the man," or "Smith," and this may, in its context, be perfectly all right; but the fact that he *is* an archaeologist may be of central importance, and we may need to emphasize his "expert knowledge of early history," or even go into further details about his specialized study. Sometimes only one facet of the meaning of a word need be shown, but sometimes that one word demands several phrases of Basic English.

Still, these three dangers are alleviated if one takes care not to commit the fourth error. One *must* compare one's Basic version critically with the original—it is not the author who is on trial, but the interpreter. It is so much the better if a number of versions can be discussed by a group of people. The original passage is the perfect version, which consists of, or contains, all the other versions. The intensive reading started with a number of questions, and this second stage, too, in the last resort, is the same thing: a number of questions—the most pointed questions one can pose about the author's meaning.

SECOND STAGE: TRANSLATE THE PASSAGE INTO BASIC ENG-
  LISH, AND COMPARE YOUR VERSIONS CLOSELY WITH THE
  ORIGINAL.

Two Basic versions of each passage are given at the

end of this chapter. There are two because I wish to emphasize the fact that there is no such thing as *the* Basic English rendering. It may be well to mention the danger of the opposite impression—that any one version is as good as any other! The chief point to be noted, however, is that each of the following versions, if symbols had been expanded fully, alternatives explored, references filled in, might well have grown into a book, which still would have provided an incomplete picture of a good intensive reading. My versions, along with the reader's own, are meant to be criticized.

Probably one should put aside the details of one's semantic theory while reading a book on other than linguistic subjects. Our knowledge about the shifts and ambiguities of sense, the powers of metaphor and abstraction, the emotional implications, and the other stratagems and devices of language will help us to read and write better, especially if we experiment with all these details ourselves, and theorize about them lengthily in our own way. But such details must not interfere with our interpretation of other matters, as they might if we tried to regiment them into a self-conscious system of interpretation. We read and write not because we want to stick semantic labels on the symbols we deal with, but in order to understand better and to live better; and the way we do these things is not separate from our purpose in doing them.

A1

1. Everybody who is interested in the well-being of society has a desire for peace. 2. This argument is only for lovers of peace, who see that most of the things valued by good and wise men are only possible where there is peace: we have no use for "those persons who are working, with an eye ever open for profit, in the military forces, in education, and in the houses of the nation's rulers, to keep us forever at war, and to put an end for all time to the free exchange of ideas." 3. Those who take the view that war will go on, because it is as necessary as food—when a truer comparison would be between war and *cannibalism,* and the time for the two of them is past—will not be profited by reading this book any further.

4. But peace is not a Buddhist heaven, where all questions of order and government are fixed and unchanging, or a *moral vacuum,* in which no decisions have to be made about good and bad, right and wrong; we would not be happy under a *peace* which put us all under the control of bad and foolish men; society has to get some way of making certain that force is used only as an instrument for good, to make all men happier and more complete. 5. Only a person of very poor quality will see much point in living simply to keep on living; if *peace* is taken in that sense, there is nothing in it of any value for us, and the old army man of history had the right idea about it.

A2

1. Every person to whom I am ready to give the name *civilized* has a desire for peace. 2. In fact, I am talking only to those who have the belief that peace is good, and that a condition of peace is possible; and who have the knowledge that most of the things which are dear to the hearts of men of good purpose are possible only in a condition of peace: we are against "those servants in the army, the university, and the government who would forever keep up physical war and keep down the war of the mind." 3. Those who are of the opinion that men will go on fighting as long as there are men, that war is as necessary to us as food—certainly food is necessary, but in the best circles it is no longer looked upon as necessary to make food of men and women like ourselves—have no need to go on reading; this book is not for them.

4. But peace is not a condition of happy unpolitical sleep, or a condition in which rules of behavior have no weight: we would not be able to go on living in a peace in which cruel, violent, and low-minded men had authority over the rest; force will have to be fixed to good purposes, and used only for good ends, based upon the best interests of all men. 5. Wise and good men are all of the opinion that to keep men safe from death is not the highest purpose of our existence: that sort of peace has not much attraction by itself, and military men through the years have been right in looking down upon it.

B1

1. Science has serious doubts about this three-angled point of view in looking at physical things. 2. Authorities of science say that when small bits of substance are looked at with care, in as much detail as is possible with the latest instruments, such substances are seen to be nothing but a complex of qualities, or sense-effects. 3. Take away a thing's qualities, and it is not possible to give any account of it, at this level. 4. But language in general is used for talking about things as we see them normally, and not as some expert sees them under special conditions. 5. Probably our language would not be so good an instrument for the common exchange of ideas if it had been made for the purposes of science. 6. It is as old as man, and men and women have made changes and additions in it when they were needed; if *orthology* (the science of language) does not keep account of this fact, and the orthologist makes out language to be something which was worked out by men of science, he will probably get into error very quickly. 7. It is not probable that the laws of language will give us much knowledge about the laws of physical existence.

B2

1. Our men of science do not see much profit in our grouping the things we see under these three general headings. 2. They say that when a physical substance is tested, and watched through a glass till its units become

so small that they are not seen even with the help of the most delicate instruments—under these conditions, the best account we are able to give of physical substances is in the language of events, not of substances; and a thing, so far as we are able to say, is nothing but a complex grouping of sense-effects, which, taken by themselves, are best named by *adjectives* (quality-words like *red, smooth, electric,* and so on). 3. The thing may be talked of only by naming its qualities. 4. But the language of everyday purposes is not the language of an expert in some special field; it is not on the same level as the language of the man of science. 5. If it had been made for such a level of discussion, probably it would not do its normal business so well. 6. It is a different instrument every time it is used, and if the language expert does not keep this fact in mind, but gets talking about language as if it had been produced by men of science, as the outcome of much thought and long testing, then the chances are that he will get on the wrong road. 7. The way our language is put together is not a good guide to the way the physical things about us are put together.

C1

1. Up to that time, psychiatry in my experience had been of little interest, and seemed to have no hopes of offering anything better for the future; though I myself was deeply interested in the processes of the mind, and had been throughout my college and university years. 2. Naturally there was enough work to be done in the

state hospital, with persons diseased in nerves or in mind, but our only instruments seemed to me to be a small number of fixed forms of words. If a young person's mind went wrong in certain ways, we said he had some form of *dementia praecox;* if the diseased person's humor went up and down regularly in certain ways, we said he had this or that form of *manic-depressive insanity;* and so it went. 3. In the Burgholzli Clinic it was quite different: we did not give a person's disease the name of this or that form of *dementia praecox*—a thing which after a little experience one was able to do at once—we gave our full attention to the special effects of such a disease, which were different with every different person. 4. In place of saying in a general sort of way that the person was hearing Fictions, we went into the question of why he was hearing his special voices or other forms of Fictions, because Freud had said that with such diseases every person has his private Fictions, and this theory was supported by all our experience. 5. They were signs of the warring forces by which his mind had been broken down.

6. At that time Jung was ready to do anything for Freud. 7. If I had had a better knowledge of the unconscious forces of the mind of which Freud first gave an account, I would have seen what the future outcome would be. 8. But now Jung would let nobody say anything against Freud's opinions; sharp and undoubting himself, he would see no other point of view. 9. He got angry with anyone who took it upon himself to put forward the

least doubt about these theories, which were certainly new and even shocking at that time. 10. Still, he did much for psychoanalysis, his strong feelings and his bright and able mind quickly putting him in the thick of the fight. 11. He was my first teacher, and I never had another with such violent feelings. 12. He was my guide while I was reading Freud's book on the connections between conscious experience and the unconscious workings of the mind in sleep.

C2

1. My experience of the medical care given to those persons who were diseased in mind had not given me much interest in this sort of work, or much belief in its future—though I myself was deeply interested in the mind and its operations, an interest which seems to have been clearly marked all through my years of higher education. 2. There had certainly been enough for me to do in the state hospital, with diseases of the nerves and mind, but all it came to was a list of names—this or that form of *dementia praecox*, or this or that form of *manic-depressive insanity*, and so on. 3. In Burgholzli we went at such questions from a different angle: we did not take the trouble of naming the person's disease—with a little experience, one was able to do this after one look at him —we were chiefly interested in how his was different from all the other conditions we had seen. 4. We did not simply say that a person had *hallucinations* of hearing; we took into account the special sorts of things he was

hearing; because, as had been pointed out by Freud, with every person these sounds and voices were different. 5. They might be used as pointers to the warring impulses responsible.

6. At that time, Jung had the strongest belief in the theories of Freud. 7. If I had had a better knowledge of Freud's discoveries, of those unconscious forces guiding the processes of the mind, I would have seen which way Jung would go in the near future. 8. But at this time he did not see how it was possible not to be in agreement with Freud's views; bright and quick of impulse, he would not see the other side. 9. He quickly became angry at anybody who did not give complete belief to Freud's theories, which after all were strange and surprising then. 10. Still, Psychoanalysis (a school of psychology based on the division of the mind into conscious and unconscious) is greatly in his debt, his burning interest and his quick and fertile brain putting him before long in the front firing line. 11. He was my first teacher, and, I may say, the teacher with the strongest feelings I ever had. 12. I went through Freud's *Traumdeutung* (The Interpretation of Dreams) under his direction.

Practice Exercises

Study at least some of the following passages intensively, in some such way as that described in the last chapter of this book: (*a*) questions, problems, and difficulties; (*b*) your idea of a Basic English version; (*c*) a close comparison of your version with the original. Can you guess the authors?

A

We've got this great industrial population, and they've got to be fed, so the damn show has to be kept going somehow. The women talk a lot more than the men, nowadays, and they are a sight more cocksure. The men are limp, they feel a doom somewhere, and they go about as if there was nothing to be done. Anyhow nobody knows what should be done, in spite of all the talk. The young ones get mad because they've no money to spend. Their whole life depends on spending money, and now they've got none to spend. That's our civilization and our education: bring up the masses to depend entirely on spending money, and then the money gives out. The pits are working two days, two and a half days a week, and there's no sign of betterment even for the winter. It means a man bringing up a family on twenty-five and thirty shillings. The women are the maddest of all. But then they're the maddest for spending, nowadays.

If you could only tell them that living and spending isn't the same thing! But it's no good. If only they were educated to live instead of earn and spend, they could manage very happily on twenty-five shillings. If the men wore scarlet trousers, as I said, they wouldn't think so much of money: if they could dance and hop and skip, and sing and swagger and be handsome, they could do with very little cash.

B

Man's advance has always been almost entirely due to the development and extension of his speech. It can be truly said that the ape became a man when he began to speak; man became civilized man when he began to write; and modern civilization dates from the invention of printing. We are now entering a new era. Lately there has been an enormous increase in the impact of words upon us; today much more is read, much more is heard than ever before, but our defenses against hurtful suggestions have not kept pace with the rapid growth of this new environment. The fact that a man can sit in a bombproof shelter and talk directly to the world has altered that world to a greater extent than did the discovery of gunpowder or the airplane. It is dislocating all our traditional behavior. We are suffering also from a large increase in our education. We are in the dangerous position of people who know a little. We know enough of the dangers that threaten us to be terrified by them. Our only defense is to know more.

C

If we wish to know how many men and women over the age of twenty live in a city, we must get every citizen to fill out a form under the headings: "male," "female," and "age." Provided every answer is correct, we can obtain, by counting and segregating them, a result of a statistical nature. The individual names and addresses on the forms are of no account. Our statistical view is gained by the knowledge of individual cases. Similarly, in the kinetic theory of matter, we have statistical laws governing the aggregation, gained on the basis of individual laws.

But in quantum physics the state of affairs is entirely different. Here the statistical laws are given immediately. The individual laws are discarded. We cannot describe the possible motion of elementary particles in space and time as we did in classical physics. Quantum physics abandons individual laws of elementary particles and states directly the statistical laws governing aggregations. It is impossible, on the basis of quantum physics, to describe positions and velocities of an elementary particle or to predict its future path as in classical physics. Quantum physics deals only with aggregations, and its laws are for crowds and not for individuals.

D

Suppose you now take this parable to the gentleman who is surprised at finding that philosophers have no honor in their cities; explain it to him and try to convince him that their having honor would be far more extraordinary.

Say to him, that, in deeming the best votaries of philosophy to be useless to the rest of the world, he is right; but also tell him to attribute their uselessness to the fault of those who will not use them, and not to themselves. The pilot should not humbly beg the sailors to be commanded by him—that is not the order of nature; neither are "the wise to go to the doors of the rich"—the ingenious author of this saying told a lie—but the truth is, that, when a man is ill, whether he be rich or poor, to the physician he must go, and he who wants to be governed, to him who is able to govern. The ruler who is good for anything ought not to beg his subjects to be ruled by him, although the present governors of mankind are of a different stamp; they may be justly compared to the mutinous sailors, and the true helmsmen to those who are called by them good-for-nothings and stargazers.

For these reasons, and among men like these, philosophy, the noblest pursuit of all, is not likely to be much esteemed by those of the opposite faction.

E

A commodity is therefore a mysterious thing, simply because in it the social character of men's labor appears to them as an objective character stamped upon the product of that labor; because the relation of the producers to the sum total of their own labor is presented to them as a social relation, existing not between themselves, but between the products of their labor. This is the reason why the products of labor become commodities, social things whose qualities are at the same time perceptible and imperceptible by the senses. In the same way the light from an object is perceived by us not as the subjective excitation of our optic nerve, but as the objective form of something outside the eye itself. But,

in the act of seeing, there is at all events an actual passage of light from one thing to another, from the external
object to the eye. There is a physical relation between
physical things. But it is different with commodities.
There, the existence of the things qua commodities, and
the value relation between the products of labor which
stamps them as commodities, have absolutely no connection with their physical properties and with the material relations arising therefrom. There it is a definite
social relation between men, that assumes, in their eyes,
the fantastic form of a relation between things.

F

I shall give an example from one of Mr. Waley's Chinese translations, to insist upon the profundity of feeling
which such a device may enshrine.

> Swiftly the years, beyond recall.
> Solemn the stillness of this spring morning.

The human mind has two main scales on which to measure time. The large one takes the length of a human life
as its unit, so that there is nothing to be done about life;
it is of an animal dignity and simplicity, and must be regarded from a peaceable and fatalistic point of view. The
small one takes as its unit the conscious moment, and it
is from this that you consider the neighboring space, an
activity of the will, delicacies of social tone, and your
personality. The scales are so far apart as almost to give
the effect of defining two dimensions; they do not come

into contact because what is too large to be conceived by the one is still too small to be conceived by the other. Thus, taking the units as a century and the quarter of a second, their ratio is ten to the tenth and their mean is the standard working day; or, taking the smaller one as five minutes, their mean is the whole of summer. The repose and self-command given by the use of the first are contrasted with the speed at which it shows the years to be passing from you, and therefore with the fear of death; the fever and multiplicity of life, as known by the use of the second, are contrasted with the calm of the external space of which it gives consciousness, with the absolute or extratemporal value attached to the brief moments of self-knowledge with which it is concerned, and with a sense of security in that it makes death so far off.

G

A great deal of ingenuity has been wasted by historians on both sides in trying to make out a good legal case. Such a case can easily be made but it is quite futile to pass judgment upon a revolution on legal grounds. The important thing is that the American bourgeoisie were growing up, and, like the English bourgeoisie of the seventeenth century, were forced by the very fact of their growth to break the barriers standing in their way. Allowing for the complicating addition of a national question, the American Revolution and the English Revolution form an almost exact parallel, both in their objects and in the forces at work. The American Revolution had its upper class leadership and its lower middle class rank and file, its internal class struggle centered mainly around the agrarian question, a struggle not finally decided till the defeat of Andrew Jackson. The war was fought mainly by the small farmers, traders, and artisans but its benefits went to the merchants and planters of whom Washington was a typical representative.

H

It is of the nature of reason to consider things as necessary and not as contingent. This necessity of things it perceives truly, that is to say, as it is in itself. But this necessity of things is the necessity itself of the eternal nature of God. Therefore it is of the nature of reason to consider things under this form of eternity. Moreover, the foundations of reason are notions which explain those things which are common to all, and these things explain the essence of no individual things, and must therefore be conceived without any relation to time, but under a certain form of eternity.

I

This is at least an obvious characteristic of all animals, for they possess a congenital discriminative capacity which is called sense-perception. But though sense-perception is innate in all animals, in some the sense-impression comes to persist, in others it does not. So animals in which this persistence does not come to be have no knowledge of objects of which no impression persists; animals in which it does come into being have perception and can continue to retain the sense-impression in the soul: and when such persistence is frequently repeated a further distinction at once arises between those which out of the persistence of such sense-impressions develop a power of systematizing them and those which do not. So out of sense-perception comes to be what we call memory, and out of frequently repeated memories of the same thing develops experience; for a number of memories constitute a single experience. From experience again—i. e. from the universal now stabilized in its entirety within the soul, the one beside the many which is a single identity within them all—originate the skill of the craftsman and the knowledge of the man of science.

J

The crucial difference between a political democracy and all other forms of government is to be found here. A democratic government is pledged to maintain a general procedure which implies the possibilities or even likelihood of its own overthrow, while an undemocratic government will use its power in whatever manner is conducive to its own perpetuation. There is no threat to political democracy in a shift of emphasis from private enterprise to public regulation, or from state to federal control, or from legislative to the executive branches of government. The diagnosticians who are watching these changes have applied their stethoscopes to the wrong spot. The enlightened guardian of democracy will scrutinize the government's attitude to its opponents and to public opinion. Does it use its power to intimidate and corrupt? Does it outlaw opposition and stifle criticism? Does it drug the public mind? Or does it rely for its possession of office on the merits of its policies as these are judged by a well-informed and free electorate? If not, then, and then only, is political democracy in jeopardy.

The purposes by which partisan liberty is justified define the limits of its toleration. If it is justified as a moral liberty, on the ground that a man naturally desires to exercise and voice his own mind, then it is limited by the principle of reciprocity. As there is no justifiable liberty of property or person which does not respect the property and persons of others, so there is no justifiable liberty of thought, speech, press, or assembly which does not respect the opinion of others and restrain itself within the bounds of temperate discussion. Whether control be exercised by public or by private agencies, the use of partisan privileges to injure the reputation or offend the honor of other individuals or groups is an intolerable abuse. Anti-Semitic propaganda, having reference to persons rather than to ideas, is a conspicuous instance of such an abuse. If it is not penalized under the laws of libel and slander, this is not because it is defensible, but only because it may be deemed inexpedient for the state to create the necessary agencies of enforcement. One thing is certain, namely, that open insult, like theft or homicide, is inconsistent with an all-embracing system of harmonious liberties.

K

All other varieties of taboo phenomena which have led to the attempted classifications noted above become unified if we sum them up in the following sentence: The basis of taboo is a forbidden action for which there exists a strong inclination in the unconscious.

We know, without understanding it, that whoever does what is prohibited and violates the taboo, becomes himself taboo. But how can we connect this fact with the other, namely, that the taboo adheres not only to persons who have done what is prohibited, but also to persons who are in exceptional circumstances, as well as to these circumstances themselves and to impersonal things? What can this dangerous attribute be which always remains the same under all these different conditions? Only one thing, namely, the propensity to arouse the ambivalence of man and to tempt him to violate the prohibition.

An individual, who has violated a taboo, becomes himself taboo because he has the dangerous property of tempting others to follow his example. He arouses envy; why should he be allowed to do what is prohibited to others? He is therefore really contagious, in so far as every example incites to imitation and, therefore, he himself must be avoided.

L

Just as in general the presumption for spiritual achievements lies in the racial quality of the given human material, thus also the individual's education has to focus upon and to promote first of all physical health; for, within the masses, a healthy, vigorous spirit will be found only in a healthy and powerful body. The fact that geniuses are sometimes physically badly formed, even sick beings, is no objection. They are the exceptions which—as everywhere—prove the rule. But if the mass of a people consists of physical degenerates, then out of this swamp a really great spirit will arise only very rarely. His activity will in no case be rewarded with great success. The degraded rabble will either not understand him at all, or it will be so weakened in its will power that it will be unable to follow the soaring flight of such an eagle.

The folkish State, through this realization, has to direct its entire education primarily not at pumping in mere knowledge, but at the breeding of absolutely healthy bodies. Of secondary importance is the training of the mental abilities. But here again first of all the development of the character, especially the promotion of will power and determination, connected with education for joyfully assuming responsibility, and only as the last thing, scientific schooling.

M

We must first inquire about definitions arising out of divisions. There is nothing in the definition except the first-named genus and the differentia. The other genera are the first genus and along with this the differentiae that are taken with it, e. g. the first may be "animal," the next "animal which is two-footed," and again "animal which is two-footed and featherless," and similarly if the definition includes more terms. And in general it makes no difference whether it includes many or few terms— nor, therefore, whether it includes few or simply two; and of the two the one is differentia and the other genus, e. g. in "two-footed animal" "animal" is genus and the other is differentia. If then the genus absolutely does not exist apart from the species which it as genus includes, or if it exists but exists as matter (for the voice is genus and matter, but its differentiae make the kinds, i. e. the letters, out of it), clearly the definition is the formula which comprises the differentiae.

But it is also necessary in division to take the differentia of the differentia; e. g. "endowed with feet" is a differentia of "animal"; again we must know the differentia of "animal endowed with feet" qua endowed with feet. Therefore we must not say, if we are to speak rightly, that of that which is endowed with feet one part has feathers and one is featherless; if we say this we say it through incapacity; we must divide it qua cloven-footed or not-cloven; for these are differentiae in the foot;

cloven-footedness is a form of footedness. And we always want to go on so till we come to the species that contain no differences. And then there will be as many kinds of foot as there are differentiae, and the kinds of animals endowed with feet will be equal in number to the differentiae. If then this is so, clearly the *last* differentia will be the substance of the thing and its definition, since it is not right to state the same things more than once in our definitions; for it is superfluous. And this does happen; for when we say "animal which is endowed with feet, and two-footed" we have said nothing other than "animal having feet, having two feet"; and if we divide this by the proper division, we shall be saying the same thing many times—as many times as there are differentiae.

N

When we have intelligence resulting from sincerity, this condition is to be ascribed to nature; when we have sincerity resulting from intelligence, this condition is to be ascribed to instruction. But given the sincerity, and there shall be the intelligence; given the intelligence, and there shall be the sincerity.

INDEX